MW01223310

More With Less

Get a Grip on Your Excessive Spending and Hoarding Habits, Create a Personalized Budget, and Adopt a Savings-Oriented Mindset and Minimalist Lifestyle

Michelle Moore

michellembooks@gmail.com

rendering medical, legal or other professional advice or services. If professional assistance is required, the services of a competent professional person should be sought. The author shall not be liable for damages arising herefrom. The fact that an individual, organization of website is referred to in this work as a citation and/or potential source of further information does not mean that the author endorses the information the individual, organization to website may provide or recommendations they/it may make. Further, readers should be aware that Internet websites listed in this work might have changed or disappeared between when this work was written and when it is read.

For general information on the products and services or to obtain technical support, please contact the author.

Table of Contents

Chapter 1: Compulsive Buying Disorder

You know that feeling when you get a really good deal? You see the price tag, double check it to make sure that it is real, and the feeling of euphoria creeps through your veins like a warm cup of coffee. It feels *great.*

My friend, Anna, absolutely lives for good deals. Black Friday is her favorite day of the year. She goes all-out for it. Honestly, Anna could probably skip Thanksgiving dinner altogether if that meant that she could start early on Black Friday. In fact, it isn't even Black Friday anymore because it starts on Thursday! Not only do you have to get in line *before* Black Friday starts, but then you have to act like you're corralling a bunch of bulls just to get that one item you really wanted.

Anna's year is divided into Black Friday preparation, Black Friday, and the giving of Black Friday gifts. She's completely normal the other days of the year, it's like she turns into a werewolf one day a year. The woman just loves to buy things that are a good deal. In fact, she loves to buy things and then gift them because they are a good deal.

You might think that Anna is a bit of a shopaholic, but that couldn't be further from the truth. She's not a shopaholic at all. If you get the shopping frenzy every once in a while, consider yourself a normal human being living in the age of consumption. Sometimes, a good deal is just too good to pass up.

However, if you find yourself buying much more than you need on a regular basis, you might want to take a step back and consider that buying things you don't need every day could be a sign of shopaholism.

Remember that movie, *Confessions of a Shopaholic*? While it is great entertainment, it isn't a great life. The main character, the kind and chatty Rebecca Bloomwood, has a serious compulsive shopping problem, yet, ironically, she works at a news agency which gives financial advice. As the movie goes on, Rebecca's life spirals lower and lower in lies, running away from debt collectors, and losing the people closest to her. Of course, in the end she turns the sinking ship around like one would expect from a cheesy Hollywood romantic comedy.

Real life doesn't work by the laws of Hollywood. The movie of the regular average Joe would go on spiraling deeper and deeper in debt and desperation. I can't promise you a Hollywood ending but I can assure you that reading this book, you'll get some down to earth advice on how to escape the vicious circle of debt, how to handle your finances better, and how to cure your compulsive shopping, hoarding, and spending habits.

Compulsive Buying Disorder (CBD)

Compulsive buying disorder (CBD) was first described as a clinical problem in the early 20th century by Bleuler and Kraepelin. "As a last category Kraepelin mentions the buying maniacs (oniomaniacs) in whom even buying is compulsive and leads to senseless contraction of debts with continuous delay of payment until a catastrophe clears the situation a little - a little bit never altogether because they never admit to their debts" says Bleuler.[i] CBD was also referred to as a "reactive impulse", or "impulsive insanity" by Bleuler, who categorized CBD together with kleptomania and pyromania.[ii]

There are many types of addictions. Alcoholism, drug abuse, and binge eating are just some of the common ones. Then there are unusual addictions like the ones shown on the show *My Strange Addiction*, like eating chalk, falling asleep to a hair dryer, and hoarding. Compulsive shopping is just as much of an addiction as the rest of them. If it isn't dealt with in a timely manner, compulsive shopping can ruin your marriage and familial relationships.

When we talk about compulsive behavior, we mean the conscious or unconscious repetition of a behavior despite adverse consequences, distress or impairment. [iii] Compulsive Buying Disorder therefore can be described as an excessive preoccupation and low impulse control with buying things. The adverse consequences of such a behavior are financial problems, spiraling into debt.

Today, around six percent of the population of the United States suffers from CBD, the majority of them being women. However, there is an increased number of men with CBD in recent years, because of the expansion and evolution of digital products. [iv]

If you compulsively shop, you have an unhealthy relationship with the act of shopping. Shopping not only gives you a relief, it can also make you anxious when you are not shopping. You would feel the constant need to purchase anything you might not necessarily want or need. This act of compulsive shopping goes far beyond the normal person's shopping habits. It interferes with your life and daily activities.

Research shows that CBD is not an independent condition. It usually is associated with other psychiatric problems such as "mood and anxiety disorders, substance use disorders, eating disorders, and other disorders of impulse control" says Donald W. Black, a psychiatrist of the University of Iowa.

While there is no research proving "shopping" personality, however, a big percentage of the people who suffer with severe CBD meet the criteria for an Axis II disorder, Black says. Axis II disorder incorporates a set number of different disorders that are considered 'personality' disorders. In other words, they affect the person's overall personality, how they relate to themselves and others.[v] There are twelve conditions, eleven personality disorders and the classification of intellectual disorders, grouped into the Axis II disorders. The entire list of Axis II disorder are the following: "personality disorders—paranoid, schizoid, schizotypal, antisocial, borderline, histrionic, narcissistic, dependent, obsessive-compulsive, personality and NOS (not otherwise specified)—and intellectual disorders, including mental retardation."[vi]

Donald W. Black argues that compulsive shopping usually runs in families that have problems with mood or substance use disorders over the generations. Often, the children learn the behavior from their parents.

Research surrounding compulsive shopping is a bit controversial because many don't believe this is truly a mental disorder. Psychopharmacologic treatment studies are actively done and it has been shown that someone who takes antidepressants can benefit from them and that they can aid in their condition. However, there is no standard, universally accepted treatment for CBD. [vii]

Those who compulsively shop get a high from buying different items. Just like when a person takes a drug, the act of shopping releases the same chemicals - like endorphins and dopamine - and gives the person a feeling of euphoria.[viii] To obtain this high, people shop over and over again, which creates a shopping addiction.

It's thought that shopping addiction affects around six percent of the United States' population alone. No one should feel ashamed if they have a shopping addiction, as you can see, you're not alone. Just like with any other addiction, those who have shopping addiction can receive help.

Shopping is cultural in the American society. It is used as a fun activity or a chance to spoil. People are introduced to this possible addiction at an early age.

Shopping itself is not illegal, so many people may not realize they have an addiction until their credit card statement arrives. Greater problems arise when people resort to criminal activity to support their level of addiction to shopping. [ix]

What makes shopping addiction – or rather getting cured from it – even more difficult is the fact that what you want to buy is readily available whenever you want. You can go online to Amazon, go to the store, or you can even use Google Home or Amazon's Alexa to order items with just your voice. It's scary that you don't even have to move an inch to buy something.

While The American Psychiatric Association doesn't currently recognize shopping addiction as a categorized disorder, there is a lot of research surrounding the problem. [x] In *The Journal of Consumer Policy*, there was a study that looked at brain scans of women with and without compulsive shopping behaviors. What the researchers found was that when the compulsive shoppers were buying something, there was a higher level of brain activity in the region that is responsible for making decisions. The Journal of Consumer Policy also found that those who compulsively shop have a higher risk of suffering from other addiction-based disorders like substance abuse, eating disorders, anxiety, and depression.[xi]

Causes and Symptoms

The causes of shopping addictions are very similar to those of other addictions. A lot of it stems from the person's childhood. Emotional trauma or being deprived of attention in your childhood could play a role in shopping addiction. Psychoanalysts have suggested that early life traumas, such as sexual abuse, could also be an underlining cause of CBD. I need to emphasize that no specific family constellation or pattern of childhood traumas has been identified as a direct cause of CBD.[xii]

There are some theories in neurobiology where experts link CBD to disturbed neurotransmitters, specifically those which have involvement with the chemicals serotonin, dopamine, and opioid systems.[xiii]

Those who seek approval and need it to survive, those who need to control things, to fill an inner void, or those who are dealing with a painful loss or grief might turn to shopping to try and numb the pain. It might start out seemingly innocent, but it is far from that.

Just because shopping isn't a drug doesn't mean that it doesn't do harm. Deep down, people with shopping addictions know this, which is why they go to such lengths to try to keep their addiction under the radar. In fact, those who compulsively shop hide it extremely well. Oftentimes, only those who are closest to the person know that there is a problem.

Why? Because you need money to shop. Compulsive shoppers often act like they have a lot of money; they show off the expensive things that they buy and act like they are really wealthy people when often they are deeply in debt. Think of shopping like swimming in the ocean. You can only tread water for so long before you go beneath the surface. The same happens with spending. Even if you start out wealthy, you can only spend and shop for so long before your wealth is gone and you're drowning in debt.

Donald W. Black observed that shopping and spending are strongly connected in most CBD cases. There are a very few who only "window shop." The first symptom Black identified talking to CBD patients was the increased urge and anxiety they felt, which only went away and got replaced by a sense of completion when the patients bought something.

In a study, Black with co-authors S. Repertinger and S. Schlosser identified four phases of CBD:

1) anticipation;

2) preparation;

3) shopping;

4) spending.[xiv]

In the anticipation phase, the CBD patient creates thoughts and urges with either purchasing a well-defined item, or with the act of shopping in general.

The second phase, preparation, includes getting ready for shopping or spending, like where to go, what to wear, how to pay and so on. This is the phase where sales and seemingly optimized shopping plans are made.

The third phase is the de facto shopping experience. This is where the person feels the most excitement. Studies show that this excitement can reach the level of the feeling of sexual arousal.[xv]

The fourth and final phase is the purchase. In this phase, people often experience a feeling of self-disappointment, sadness, anxiety of their instable finances, the pink shopping bubble pops, in other words. Excessive research proves that depression, anxiety, boredom, self-critical thoughts, and anger were the most frequently mentioned antecedents to compulsive shopping. Euphoria or relief from the negative emotions are the most common consequence.[xvi]

Another symptom of CBD can be the company or lack of company of the compulsive shopper. To avoid embarrassment and shame, people with buying disorder do conclude their shopping tours as a solitary activity unless they have someone in their close circle who is also a compulsive shopper.

CBD is not related to a person's income. Anyone can develop this condition from the upper one percent to the least wealthy. The shopping shrines usually vary based on the budget of someone. Those with a seven-figure income can go crazy in a garage sale and in Louis Vuitton just the same, while those with a tight budget usually shop in low-cost places. The most common items bought as a consequence of compulsive shopping are clothes, accessories, shoes, cosmetic items, home décor products and such. Among men, the most common shopping items are watches, car accessories, audio-visual devices, mobile phones, gaming-related purchases, and electronic hobby tools.[xvii]

A study conducted by S. Schlosser showed that most of the people affected are aware, and able to admit that they have a shopping problem, and that they feel a lot of anxiety because of their financial situation.[xviii] Other studies concluded that almost seventy percent of people who have CBD experienced relationship deterioration with their closest loved ones. An even higher percentage of ninety-two tried to resist their shopping temptations, however, seventy-two percent of them couldn't keep his or her pledge.[xix]

Collectively, the common symptoms of CBD are the following:

- Obsessing over shopping daily or weekly.
- Maxing out credit cards.
- Opening up new credit cards without paying off your previous ones.
- When stressed, your first reaction is to go and shop.
- Feeling very excited or euphoric once you purchase something.
- Buying items that aren't necessary and often never get used.
- Feeling guilty or regretful over the purchases you make, *but you're unable to stop purchasing.*

- Stealing or lying to those closest to you.
- Failing most of the time you try to stop your shopping.[xx]

You don't need to feel embarrassed if you identify yourself as a compulsive shopper, but you should try to seek help. The first step to stopping your compulsive shopping habit is to admit you have a problem. This sounds simple, but in fact it is so hard! It's like trying to admit to your partner that you are wrong. It's like something eats at your insides, but once you get it done, you'll feel *so* much better.

Once you admit that you have a problem, it's time to seek help. The best and most effective help is a counselor or a mental health professional specialized in addictions. These people are trained to help you to the best of their abilities, and you'll have the greatest chance to successfully get your shopping under control. A therapist can help you identify *the triggers* of your shopping addiction, how to avoid them, and how to control your impulses. [xxi]

As you read above, shopping addiction often stems from deeper issues. Seeing a therapist can help you determine what other possible psychiatric comorbidity can lie beneath the surface. These trained professionals can help you see what is wrong, and a psychiatrist can prescribe a treatment, and/or medication to treat the underlying issue. Treating the main cause could help eliminate the shopping addiction as well.

There are also self-help groups that are great to aid in your recovery. Shopaholics Anonymous is a good example, and there are often both in-person groups and online groups that can help you attain a sense of community. This is a problem many people struggle with, and it can be helpful to surround yourself with others who are also in recovery.

The treatment for shopping addictions should interrupt your addiction cycle by helping you to face the issue head-on, and develop new ways to deal with your triggers and react in a healthy way. There are many resources out there that can help you. There are money management classes, and 12-step recovery programs that aim to treat shopping addiction and get rid of it for good.

Here is a short list of resources where you can get help – for free or a smaller amount of money:

- Spenders Anonymous: http://www.spenders.org/list.html
- Debtors Anonymous: https://www.debtorsanonymous.org
- Better Help: www.betterhelp.com
- + Support Groups: https://shopping-addiction.supportgroups.com

If you are a chain smoker, you have the possibility to commit to stop smoking and then indeed, never touch a cigarette again. The case of shopping is different. You can't stop shopping completely because you have to buy food, clothes, cosmetics and other necessities. You can ask your spouse or friends to do the shopping while you are recovering but let's face it, not making a single purchase until the end of your life is not a realistic option. But you can always get rid of your credit cards. While you're recovering from addiction, it can help to only use cash. That way, it will be difficult to go over your limit and you can still buy the things you need. When you need to shop, do it in-store with two crutches: a list and a friend. You might feel like you've failed while you're in recovery because you are still shopping.

Avoid online shopping sites and TV shopping channels like the plague. Those are the things that can lead you to a relapse and downward spiral.

Who needs a fifth set of Magic Knives or a massage chair anyway? If you can, just block these channels or unsubscribe from them.

Making purchases for essential items can happen every day, but you have to learn how to control your urges. Depending on how severe your addiction is, you may need someone to help control the finances for a while. If you're married, you could have your spouse do the shopping and control the finances. If you are not married, talk to a friend or a professional financial advisor to help sort out your money and control where your money is going. I know, I know, it is hard to feel like you're being cut off from your own money. Think of it as a long-term benefit, an investment. You'll end up having more money and less stress this way.

Untreated Shopping Addiction

Seeking out help for an addiction can be scary, but not receiving treatment is even scarier. There are some serious consequences you can incur if you leave your addiction untreated. You have seen what happens with those who have severe drug or alcohol addictions. These people spiral into a web of lying and stealing from their closest loved ones. They end up without family to go home to, and a raging addiction. It seems so obvious to the ones outside of the situation that their addicted loved one should just quit and become better, but for those who are in the middle of the addiction, things are not that simple. Many of CBD patients see the world through a different lens, where each purchase is deeply rationalized and justified – especially in their moment of frenzy. They can see shopping as a haven and the loved one who wants to "take this haven away" could easily end up being the enemy.

When you are on the other side, the loved one who wants to help his or her friend or spouse with shopping disorder, you need to use some tact. Making your friend or spouse feel attacked and criticized won't help your cause; neither will it help them. Try to restrain yourself from direct finger pointing. Don't mix your observation about their behavior with evaluation.[xxii] Sentences like "oh, you're shopping again" or "you lack control so much when it comes to shopping" clearly deliver a message of criticism. Consequently, the CBD affected person will become defensive and non-cooperative. "I observed that this was the fifth shopping tour you had this week." This way you are stating a pure observation without finger pointing, and you have a better chance of being listened to afterwards.

If you just recognized that someone around you has a shopping addiction but has no clue about it, the best you can do is make her or him aware of the problem. Some people don't even realize they have this addiction. As a friend or relative, you should help them recognize their unhealthy behavior. But be careful; people don't like to be wrong or criminalized. If they feel attacked, people will become defensive and deny everything.

Be smart about it. First, decriminalize the situation. Tell your shopaholic friend about compulsive shopping in the third person, as if you have another friend who does it. Or just talk about it as if you have read a newspaper article about it. Sometimes, that's enough to make your friend realize she might have an issue.

If that's not enough, slowly start pointing out — preferably at the moment it's happening — when the shopaholic friend is "in action." Ask kindly but firmly, "Do you really need that shirt?" Or,

"What about leaving this pair of shoes here and think about it until tomorrow?" Being caught in the moment leaves no space for denial or defense.

If someone is aware of their shopping addiction, it is easier to communicate and help them, of course. Try to help with some of the techniques mentioned in this chapter — by suggesting financial aid, a good behavioral therapy office, or simply offering to listen.

Shopping addictions can ruin a person's life. Shopping requires spending, and those who compulsively shop can easily find themselves in debt. Money isn't the only thing one could lose, though. They lose their loved ones' trust because of the lack of consideration for their wellbeing. If someone with shopping addiction has a family, each member will suffer the consequences of an empty wallet. I generally encourage people to think about and love themselves first. In case of addictions, I say, if you don't care about how you will end up being, at least think about the people who love you and who are dear to you. When one harms himself, he harms everyone who loves him.

After a long period of misery, even the most loving heart will get fed up with hardships she isn't causing. It's frustrating, and she might end up getting to a point where she just wants to stop being together with the person who has an addiction because it hurts too bad. If you persist with your shopping addiction, you might end up losing the people dearest to you. Stop trading valuable people for valueless stuff.

Get help, and get happy.

Chapter 2: The Psychology of Hoarding

I went to visit my grandma. When I arrived to her house, she was sitting on her chair in the living room and she informed me she was moving. I congratulated both her and my grandpa for buying a new home. She was so excited that I couldn't say no when she asked me to help her move.

My grandparents are in great shape for their age, and they were going to move the majority of their things by themselves with the help of me and my family, and their neighbors. I remember thinking, "How much stuff can these two people have?" I figured I would swing on by that Saturday and help them out for an hour or two and then we'd be on our way to the new house.

At the end of the day Saturday, I looked at the house, back to the moving trucks (yes, I said *trucks*, not truck!), back to the house, and back to the trucks. I was hot, sweaty, and I could not understand how so much came out of that house. Things just kept on coming. It was like one of those clown cars that can somehow fit twenty clowns. They just had *so* much *stuff.*

I understand where my grandparents are coming from. Their parents grew up during the Great Depression, and so my grandparents were told that they needed to save everything they had because the world could collapse again. They took that advice literally.

Hoarding behavior can escalate to be a real issue. Most hoarders don't realize that they're holding onto things. I could point out everything that is not needed to a hoarder and they would practically laugh in my face. Unawareness is the problem. My grandparents knew they were holding onto their items and that they had a lot of stuff. They were *aware* of it. And yet, they still did it.

Compulsive hoarding until recently has been considered a symptom within OCD (obsessive-compulsive disorder), but in 2013, the American Psychiatric Association in The Diagnostic and Statistical Manual of Mental Disorders – 5th Edition (DSM-5) categorized Hoarding Disorder as a separate problem. Based on the DSM-5, the International OCD Association presents the main characteristics of Hoarding Disorder the following way:

- "Persistent difficulty discarding or parting with possessions, regardless of their actual value.
- This difficulty is due to a perceived need to save the items and to distress associated with discarding them.

- The difficulty discarding possessions results in the accumulation of possessions that congest and clutter active living areas and substantially compromises their intended use. If living areas are uncluttered, it is only because of the interventions of third parties (e.g., family members, cleaners, authorities).

- The hoarding causes clinically significant distress or impairment in social, occupational, or other important areas of functioning (including maintaining a safe environment for self and others).

- The hoarding is not attributable to another medical condition (e.g., brain injury, cerebrovascular disease, Prader-Willi syndrome).

- The hoarding is not better explained by the symptoms of another mental disorder (e.g., obsessions in obsessive-compulsive disorder, decreased energy in major depressive disorder, delusions in schizophrenia or another psychotic disorder, cognitive deficits in major neurocognitive disorder, restricted interests in autism spectrum disorder)."[xxiii]

Scientists observed that even if hoarding disorder doesn't meet the criteria for hoarding disorder comorbidity, people who suffer from OCD often show hoarding symptoms.[xxiv]

When we think about Hoarding Disorder we usually imagine lonely adults and war-worn elderly – like my grandparents – being the main "perpetrators." Research shows that young children can just as much show hoarding symptoms. Hoarding Disorder is not that obvious with children because adults can control and moderate it. Some children (as far I can recall, myself included) have difficulty discarding old, broken toys, clothing, and even items of little value, such as the Christmas wrapping paper, parts of the Christmas tree (I still have a little box of a piece of the branches of each Christmas tree), empty pens and such. Within children, these items hold a sentimental value and, considering that for a child of five to ten, almost each of such items can be related to a new, pleasant experience in their lives, it is understandable where their hoarding need is coming from. [xxv]

Children often attribute human traits to their non-living items. While anthropomorphism can be outgrown with time, make sure to address the feeling of incompleteness or the fear (of never experiencing the happiness the preserved token represents) your child nonverbally communicates. The need to preserve memories is one of the most common OCD symptoms related to hoarding. [xxvi]

Talk to your child. Make sure he or she understands that in a lifetime, people have many happy memories and keeping a memory of each of them is simply unsustainable. In today's modern age, it is possible to take a photo of everything. Try to bargain a deal with your child to make photographic memories of the cherished items instead of actual ones. Untreated Hoarding Disorder present in childhood can easily go on in adulthood. If as a child someone learns that the way to preserve happiness is through keeping things related to the memory, they subconsciously might do the same as adults. The rates of hoarding are estimated to be anywhere from 2-5% of the adult population. The symptoms worsen as someone ages, usually peaking in older adults when family members have moved away or died, leaving a huge void that people with Hoarding Disorder try to fill up with even more things. [xxvii]

Hoarding Disorder is often excessive, and its byproduct(s) cover the living areas of the home. Because of this, hoarding causes significant distress to both the person hoarding and those living with the hoarder. Hoarding comes with its own fair share of health risks, financial burdens, and relationship strain. While hoarders could be aware that their behavior is irrational, they still cannot throw away the items in the house. It is a relatively new problem because people in the past may not have had the space, time, or resources to hoard items.[xxviii]

Because of its relative newness, researchers have just started to study hoarding, why it happens, and the reasons behind it. Hoarding can be a mental disorder of its own, but it can also have underlying causes like other psychological disorders including depression, anxiety, and ADHD.[xxix]

OCD and Hoarding

There is relationship between OCD and hoarding. While many individuals with OCD may compulsively hoard, not all people who hoard have OCD. If a person compulsively hoards, there are three symptoms they will all demonstrate. According to the International OCD Foundation, compulsive hoarders will collect and keep many different items that may not be usable or have little value, their items will cover much-needed living spaces and can keep a person from using their own room in their house, and the items they are keeping cause problems throughout the day.

Research shows that about 25% of people with OCD compulsively hoard, and only 5-20% of hoarders have symptoms of OCD. [xxx] Individuals who hoard that may have OCD will often show symptoms of their hoarding being driven by fear or superstition. Their own hoarding behavior will be frustrating and unwanted, and they probably won't show interest in the items they hoard. Hoarding in and of itself does not incite the same activity in the brain displayed in individuals who have OCD.

Alberto Petrusa et al. in their article *"Compulsive Hoarding: OCD Symptom, Distinct Clinical Syndrome, or Both?"* presented two cases of Hoarding Disorder, one where the patient didn't have OCD related to her hoarding and one where the patient had previously been diagnosed with OCD. Here are the stories:

    a.) Ms. S' case of compulsive hoarding syndrome without OCD

Ms. S worked as a secretary, she was single, fifty-one years old. She admitted that she always felt hesitation and hardship when she needed to part from an item. Since she's been like this forever, she didn't consider her condition to be special or problematic.

For a few years she started feeling cramped in her flat since it became very cluttered. On one hand, she felt that she should get rid of some of the objects, on the other hand, she felt a strong resistance to take action on her gut feeling. She feared she might trash something important (like paperwork) or something sentimentally valuable and unrepeatable. She felt safer surrounded by her things.

While her bathroom and kitchen were relatively accessible, her living room and bedrooms were so cluttered that she didn't dare invite anyone over for a couple years. She felt embarrassed. Her social life was not great as a consequence which led her to becoming depressed.

When she reached out to mental health specialists, she thought she had some kind of OCD, however, the doctors could not agree whether she had OCD. The only OCD symptom Ms. S. showed was her hoarding. She didn't have any repetitive obsessive behavior related to her hoarding either. She described her feelings being mainly in harmony with and consistent with her ideal self-image. Psychology calls this egosyntonic behavior. When clutter started to have an obvious negative toll on her life, Ms. S independently reached out for help.[xxxi]

b.) Ms. P's case of compulsive hoarding as a symptom dimension of OCD

Ms. P was diagnosed with prototypical OCD when she was sixteen years old. The OCD symptoms she had were fear of contamination and checking among others. At that age she still didn't have hoarding symptoms.

At the age of forty-four she went through a divorce and, as a consequence, she started feeling a profound anxiety whenever she had to part from an item. This condition worsened over the years, reaching a point where she refused to discard anything, including her body products like her nails and feces.

When people tried to help her and asked her to get rid of these things, she felt overwhelming anxiety. Whenever someone forced her to throw out something, she had to look at the item in question long enough to be able to memorize how it looked. Afterwards, when she went to bed, she regularly recalled every discarded item with a richness of details to preserve the cherished memory forever.

The obsessive fear of loss and hoarding affected every aspect of Ms. P's life. Her experience was egodystonic, meaning her thoughts and behaviors were in conflict with the needs and goals of her ideal self-image.[xxxii][xxxiii]

Hoarding does not respond well to medication. While medication may reduce some of the symptoms, it won't take away all that is there. The research of Arthur L. Brody M.D et al. in their paper *"Cerebral Glucose Metabolism in Obsessive-Compulsive Hoarding"* showed that patients with compulsive hoarding syndrome as an OCD symptom "had a different pattern of cerebral glucose metabolism than nonhoarding OCD patients and comparison subjects." They concluded that obsessive-compulsive hoarding could be considered as a neurobiologically distinct subgroup of OCD who, due to poor response to anti-obsessional treatment, should be treated by lowering the activity in the cingulate cortex."[xxxiv]

Causes of Hoarding

Hoarding is a psychological issue, but how does it happen? A packrat doesn't wake up one day and suddenly become a hoarder. It is a process that can take a while, and professionals aren't entirely sure what causes hoarding.

A person's personality could also play into the cause of hoarding. Research has shown that hoarders are very indecisive people who exhibit signs and symptoms of anxiety. And while hoarding isn't passed on through the generations, there could be something to the idea that your genes may predispose you to be a hoarder. [xxxv]

Hoarding is often used as a coping mechanism for many people. Those who hoard usually experienced a traumatic event that kicked the hoarding into gear. Once they begin to hoard, they usually feel alone and withdrawn from the rest of society, which then causes them to hoard more. The more stress that a hoarder feels, the more the boxes start to pile up.

Wouldn't it be great if we could flip a switch and suddenly the hoarding tendencies were gone? As much as we might wish for that, it isn't feasible. The first step to getting rid of hoarding is seeking treatment. Diagnoses of hoarding often occur when someone seeks out treatment for another disorder they have, like anxiety or depression.

The therapist or psychiatrist will ask the patient about his or her different disorders, and then may ask about collecting, acquiring, and saving habits. This often leads to the discussion on hoarding. Going through the DSM-5, a mental health professional will ask diagnostic questions and try to determine if someone exhibits symptoms of hoarding in addition to the other disorders they are seeking help for. If they do receive a hoarding diagnosis, it is important to seek out a therapist or psychiatrist who has had experience dealing with hoarding in the past. [xxxvi]

Hoarding is a complex problem because most people don't recognize the impact that hoarding is having on their daily lives. Failing to see an issue there, people affected by Hoarding Disorder probably don't think they need any treatment. Plus, hoarding isn't something that receiving medication can fix. It is a problem with roots deep in the psyche, which is why treatment is often limited to psychotherapy.

Cognitive behavioral therapy (CBT) is the most commonly used form of psychotherapy for hoarding treatment. This can be done through any mental health professional who is experienced in dealing with hoarding behavior. Cognitive behavioral therapy (CBT) is commonly referred to as "talk therapy," so there is nothing to be afraid of. These therapists aim to help the patient reduce the symptoms of saving and acquiring items, and they deal with the underlying issues. Going to therapy can help the patient learn how to resist the urge to keep things, and it can help improve their coping skills so they can go through the items in their house and decide what to keep and what to discard.

Finding the right motivation to change can help improvement and recovery. Family and friends should be included in the treatment program so the person affected by Hoarding Disorder can find the motivation to stop the problem in its tracks. This can also improve the social life of the patient - bonding with their loved ones.

One should remember that the treatment progress will come and go like waves. There will be times one might not feel like they are making progress, and times where he or she will be frustrated and at a loss for what to do during treatment. It is hard work but it's worth the effort. Over time, CBT can greatly reduce the amount of hoarding in one's life.[xxxvii]

There are other assistance programs that can help you beyond the regular treatment. People with Hoarding Disorder could consider looking for local resources where they can connect with others who may be going through the same issue as them. When they start to feel like they can get rid of some of the items they have accumulated over time, there are many professional organizers who can get help for them in a timely manner. It can help to step away from the house while others help to organize and discard their things.

Here are some organizations that can help you with your physical or mental hoarding problems:

- Alliance – environmental group Llc.: https://www.alliance-enviro.com/services/trauma-cleanup/hoarding-cleanup/
- Hoarding Cleanup: https://www.hoardingcleanup.com
- The Hoarding Project: http://thehoardingproject.org/groups

- International OCD Foundation: https://hoarding.iocdf.org/professionals/treatment-of-hoarding-disorder/

-

Perhaps the most important home treatment is self-care. Cleaning bathrooms and kitchens can be a good start to be able to start the process of self-care. Hygiene is extremely important to keep one healthy. Eating healthy, nutritional food in one's own kitchen is another good form of self-care. [xxxviii]

All of these practices lead to small victories one can celebrate every day. When people focus on the many small steps, they find themselves standing on a hill of victory sooner than expected.

Chapter 3: Spending Habits

We can all aim to spend a little less money. Not only does it keep us afloat in life, but it also helps keep our house clear of clutter. We're blessed to live in the day and age that we do, but this blessing doesn't come without its challenges. Overspending is something the majority of the population deals with, but it doesn't have to make your life difficult any longer.

The Causes of Overspending

Many reasons can lie behind overspending habits. For one, credit cards are readily available these days. You can't go to a retail store without being asked if you would like to sign up for the store credit card since you get a discount. Many people fall prey to these tactics, which leads to a sad, negative budget balance at the end of the month. This issue can be fixed without requiring any psychological assistance, and in the following chapters, I will try to help you overcome your bad spending habits by providing attractive and easy budgeting methods and an alternative lifestyle which is more sustainable.

In the U.S. alone, there's over $600,000,000,000 in credit card debt and upwards of 15,000,000 people who are addicted to spending. Yes, there are lots of zeros there. Those who do have a spending addiction do anything it takes to get what they want. Since credit cards are so easy to obtain, you might feel invincible and like you could go on forever by obtaining a new credit card. This couldn't be further from reality. [xxxix]

If compulsive or impulsive spending is connected to a deep psychological cause, the problem is harder to overcome. Spending addiction may occur for the following reasons:

- trying to cope with a sense of emptiness,
- need for stimulation,
- perfectionism,
- avoidance to face and cope with negative emotions,
- deprivation experienced earlier in life,
- compulsion or impulsivity,
- coping with loss or abandonment.

I discussed many aspects of shopping addiction or compulsive buying disorder in Chapter 1. In this chapter I will focus more on the financial consequences of overspending.

Someone who has an addiction usually needs a sense of control. When someone gets to purchase anything they want without consequences, they experience instant gratification, they feel in control, and it is a stress-reliever. It can help mask the symptoms of depression or anxiety. But, that's the best part one will get from overspending. *A painkiller.* Eventually, you'll have to deal with the negative feelings you are experiencing. And with a negative credit card balance.

Not everyone who shops has a spending addiction. Many of us get spending urges that are short-lived. However, if you don't recognize what you're doing when you're spending, the urges can become something permanent.

Retail Therapy

The first urge many of us get is retail therapy. I was dating someone for a while, and it didn't work out like I thought it was going to. The first urge I got was to go shopping. This had been ingrained in my mind since *forever*. When your partner dumps you, going to the mall, buying things you craved for so long seems like an obvious choice.

Shopping makes people feel good for a short period of time. It is comforting. The problem with retail therapy is it only provides temporary relief from dysphoria, yet the things one buys cost money. When reality hits us after the shopping frenzy, we might want to go back for more and purchase again to get that good feeling. A study conducted at Youngstown State University found that women are more likely to participate in retail therapy (64% of women vs. 40% of men). [xl]

Impulse Buying

Going back to my friend who loves Black Friday shopping, there was one year she bought an Xbox. Anna wasn't into playing video games, but when she saw how good of a deal she could get on the console, she bought it without giving it a second thought. Nowadays, the Xbox is collecting dust on her TV stand.

Impulse buying doesn't have to be pricey items like an Xbox, but what you buy can still leave its mark on your finances. Buying small chocolates in the checkout line, grabbing snacks from vending machines, and other low-cost purchases can still add up. Impulse buying is when you go to the store, and plan to buy bread yet you leave with two bags of things.

Experts made an important distinction between impulse buying and compulsive shopping. Their difference lies in one's motivation for making the purchase. The former is an unplanned shopping activity and kicks in the moment someone sees something attractive or desirable. Thus, impulse buying is a reaction to an external stimulus.

Compulsive shoppers do not buy on impulse. Their shopping experience is largely planned with the specific purpose to avoid pain or create pleasure to escape a negative emotion like anxiety. Compulsive shoppers are more likely to run into financial distress and emotional hardship.

Compulsive shopping can turn into an addiction easier than impulse shopping because compulsive shoppers deliberately plan out their experience with the purpose of getting rid of stress and other negative feelings.[xli]

This being said, I'm not trying to imply that impulse buying is a normal habit. However, if that's the only bad spending habit you have, the solution to overcome it might be easier. On one hand, questioning yourself before impulsively buying an item could help. "Do I really need this? How often would I use this item?" If self-questioning didn't help, you can intentionally keep the price tag on the product so you can return it the next day. Some call the process of impulse buying – returning cycle a shopping bulimia. However, if it doesn't happen too often it's just a mild shopping indigestion.

The University of British Columbia and the Cheung Kong Graduate School of Business conducted a study and found that impulse spending is usually associated with disorganized environments. This means that impulse buying happens when someone is surrounded by chaos. It actually affects your brain to react in a normal way, so something you wouldn't normally buy suddenly looks like a great idea. [xlii]

Solutions to Overspending

Retail Therapy

To stop indulging in retail therapy, you have to get to know yourself a little. Retail therapy is usually spurred on by emotions, so one needs to see what their triggers are. Some people might engage in retail therapy when they are sad, while others will engage in retail therapy because they are angry. If someone is feeling especially happy, they might spend as well. The motivation for spending is a completely individual process, so you have to see what it is for you.

To find out what your triggers are, you'll need to track your spending for a while. You can do this by saving your receipts, or use an app on your phone to track it (which I think is the better option, so you aren't hoarding fifty different pieces of paper). Once you go through your spending, you should try identifying a spending pattern.

Discovering your triggers is the first step. Then you have to find a way to reduce your emotional spending. I personally love what is called the two-day rule.

Before you go to the store, write down everything you think you need. Once you get there, only shop for those items on your list. If you find that you want something that isn't on your list, write it down with the price in your phone. Then give yourself two days to think about the item you wanted but didn't think you needed before you entered the store. In the two days, think about whether you actually need that item. Be honest. If you know you don't need it but you like it very much, you can still treat yourself with it. But create a "cost" for it. Let's say you want to buy a jacket. Sure, do it, but then get rid of another jacket. One piece comes, one piece goes.

In addition to this rule, you should do a huge "spring cleaning" of your phone and email. Delete all those shopping apps on your phone that give you notifications five times a day. Not only are they annoying, but they lure you in with the promise of sales. Remember, even if something is on sale, you didn't save money — you spent exactly as much money as the item cost.

Unsubscribe to all of the different stores you have subscribed to over the years. A great way to do this is to use the app called *Unroll Me* - https://unroll.me. The app will unsubscribe you from all of these different stores in just a few minutes so you don't have to spend all your time doing so.

You need to learn to budget (which I will talk about later). You could find a budget buddy. This is a friend or loved one who can help you stick to your budget when you get that itch to spend some money. Talking to someone can help you reduce the feeling of wanting to overspend.

Impulse Buying

Impulse buying is not the way to relieve the stress in your life. Clear your mind and try to shake out that stress. You can literally try to shake it out (sometimes just moving your body makes you feel better!), or you could try taking a few slow breaths.

Bring yourself back to base. The trick to beat impulse buying is to think about it. Taking a few slow breaths will buy you some time to get conscious about your buying urge and take the appropriate measures to stop yourself from undermining your monthly budget – again.

Before making the purchase, ask yourself if the object will enrich your life in any way. Is the item helping you to achieve your most important goals? Be honest with yourself — don't try to sell yourself.

If the questions don't work, use some good old economics, drop the "opportunity cost" bomb into the picture. Opportunity cost is the loss of other alternatives when you choose another. What's the price of the desired item? Try to come up with at least three things that cost the same amount of money – or less – which would certainly enrich your life more.

You can also calculate how much "lifetime and energy" does the desired product cost you. Divide your monthly income with the number of hours you work a month to get your hourly wage (in case you don't know it yet). Memorize this number. The next time you want to buy something impulsively, recall how much "lifetime and energy" you spend on that product. In other words, how many hours do you need to work for it? Is this item still worth that much of your life?

Money Disorder

Today, everything material and, above that, experiences with our loved ones, can be purchased for money – thus money can be considered our indirect source for happiness. At the same time, money – or rather the lack of it – can lead to profound misery as well. Research showed that financial disagreements and problems are the leading cause for divorce in the first few years of marriage. Also, seventy-two percent of the American population considers money as the number one stress factor in their lives.[xliii] Other negative consequences of money misery can lead to depression, emotional problems, anxiety, poor focus, and other mental and physical issues. Psychologist Klontz Brad assesses that "with record high debt and record low savings rates in the years leading up to the economic crisis, the average American seemed to suffer from a money disorder." He diagnoses money disorder as being a "persistent pattern of self-destructive and self-limiting financial behavior."[xliv]

Klontz states that people who have traumatic memories related to money (which he calls "flashpoints") can carry these memories deep into their adulthood. These traumas are usually the building bricks of one's financial problems. Financial traumas can stem from as early as childhood. Someone who lacked greatly or lived in poverty as a child, having parents who often argued about finances, could easily adopt negative patterns in relation to money. Finding the root cause for money misery is the first step to healing and developing a better relationship with money.

People having a strong negative opinion about money hold some negative beliefs and convictions to it. By admitting that one's relationship with money is bad, it can lead to learning, to identify the destructive beliefs with money, question them, revise them, and ultimately change them. In his book, *Mind Over Money*, Klotz talks about different categories of money disorder.[xlv]

The first category he identifies is called "Money Avoidance Disorder." People who belong here are either in financial denial or a financial rejection.

Financial denial is when someone doesn't want to face his or her financial reality. They don't think about their money problems together. They'd rather think of each financial issue individually – or try not thinking of them at all – to make their problems seem smaller in their minds.

Financial rejection happens when someone – especially with low self-esteem – accumulates a larger sum of money but can't identify with it. Either they spend it to get back to the mental comfort zone of their "net worth" or they struggle internally, developing a high level of anxiety because of the money.

The second category of Klotz's is Money-Worshipping Disorder. People with hoarding disorder, compulsive buyers, and gamblers belong to this category. For those with hoarding disorder, accumulating items – or money like Uncle

Scrooge – gives a sense of security, and temporary relief of anxiety.

For compulsive buyers, spending money feels like a blessing while the purchase is made and a curse after the dopamine, generated by the shopping-high, clears out of their system. Then they will crave another round of their favorite chemical. Gamblers function based on the same system.

The third category presented in *Mind Over Money* is "Relational Money Disorder." People within this category experience financial dependence of some sort. The author differentiates financial infidelity and financial enabling.

Financial infidelity means telling white or darker lies to one's spouse or family members, making binge purchases outside of the established budget. This can be from as mild an issue as buying new accessories for the finishing set to extreme problems as taking money out unilaterally from the common savings account, taking out a second mortgage and so on.

Financial enabling usually occurs in cases of parents who support their grown-up children, making them dependent on this aid. This behavior often deprives the adult child of learning to be independent and taking care of him or herself. Not to mention that the parent might give to the child, sacrificing his or her own financial wellbeing.

Overcoming money disorders doesn't have to be complicated. First, one has to identify what category of money disorder he or she falls in, collect the main traumas related to that category, and then question the money beliefs he or she has. To do all this, it's better to use specialists. First, a counselor to pin down the psychology-related problems and later, a financial advisor to build up a tailor-made, doable budget to accumulate a healthy amount of savings, get clear of debt, and create a smart spending plan.

As Klontz Brad says, aim to become emotionally wealthier as well, not only materially.

Chapter 4: Budgeting Methods

Budgeting isn't as scary as it sounds. It is creating a spending plan that will help determine how much money one needs to live, and how much he or she can spend on other things.

Budgeting is important for everyone. It can help manage money and plan for the future. In an optimal world, we'd make more money than we are spending. In reality, many people don't realize they are actually spending more than they make. Whether they want to stay out of debt or rid themselves of existing debt, creating a budget will help do these things so they become less anxious and ready to take on life.

Money is a source of many emotions, and budgeting creates a plan to have enough money to live on. When you know exactly where your money is going, you suddenly feel that a huge weight has been lifted off of your shoulders. Once you start budgeting, you can determine which months are your highs and which months are your lows. No one is going to have exactly two months the same because there are holidays, birthdays, seasonal expenses, etc. that need to be paid at different times of the year. The goal is to have extra money on those high months so that you can afford to live through your low months.

Getting Started

Step one is to track your income and expenses.

Take the leap and track all of your past spending history. This includes your bills, your card statements, your grocery bills, eating out receipts

— everything. It can take a bit of time to do this tracking, and you'll want to make sure you follow at least a full month's worth of transactions. You need to know all the symptoms to make a proper diagnosis. Imagine if a doctor would diagnose you based on only one or two things, "hmm, headache and dizziness, this could be either a common end-of-the-day fatigue or… leprosy." You know, those two symptoms match either condition. They require different treatment though.

Step two is figuring out your monthly average income and spending.

Add up everything you have earned for the past twelve months and all of your expenses for the past twelve months. You can find most of this by looking at your bank statements.

Step three is to determine your monthly revenue history.

For those who are in a salaried position, this is easy because your revenue will be the same each month. However, for those who are paid hourly or freelance, this is a bit more difficult calculus. A year's worth of income is the best income metric for those who are paid hourly or work as freelancers. This is because you don't usually have two months that are the same.

Remember that what you are bringing home is your income before taxes are taken out. You'll need to know your annual income so you can figure out how much you will owe in taxes when the time comes. Subtract your taxes from your income. If you are in a salaried position, don't put your tax return into the amount of money you make a year. These are far too unreliable and change too often.

Step four is writing down all of your monthly expenses.

This is more than your gas and electric bill. You should include your rent or mortgage, car insurance, loan payments, health insurance, eating out, grocery bills, monthly movies with friends, those happy hour charges you rack up on Friday nights, and your shopping charges. You probably underestimate how much you spend per month. Double- and triple-check everything you have written down. It is far too easy to forget something – be sure that you have an accurate number of how much you spend per month.

Step five is analyzing.

Get ready to take a closer look at your revenue and expenses. The two numbers should be unbalanced, hopefully to the favor of revenues. However, too many of us end up spending way beyond our means. This happens whenever your expenses are more than your revenue. Let's see what kind of expenses can you have?

Fixed expenses are regular monthly expenses that you have to pay all the time. Your bills, insurance, debts, and groceries are all part of these fixed expenses. It is basically everything that you *have* to buy to survive or to avoid having a debt collector breaking down your door.

Discretionary expenses could be considered optional expenses. Things like eating out or getting your hair done every few weeks could be slashed from your budget if you are spending more money than you make.

Set Up Your Budget

Setting up your budget is your first step to financial freedom. Look at it as a step that is going to make you better off in the long run.

First things first, set up your <u>fixed expenses</u> in a budget. Like I mentioned earlier, you need to find the average you pay for a month of living. This includes everything you absolutely have to pay like loan payments and power bills. However, since these bills vary from month to month, you are taking an average. When you set up your budget, add about five to ten percent to everything you put down. For example, if you pay $100 for water, put your budget as $105-$110. This gives you a little bit of extra cushion just in case something unexpected happens.

Hopefully, you'll have some money left over after paying your fixed expenses. What you do with that money is up to you, but it is smart to set some goals and write those into your budget. These goals can be anything from saving up for a vacation, to something as big as putting aside a few thousand dollars in an emergency savings account.

Whatever your goal is, make it SMART.

SMART is an abbreviation for Specific, Measurable, Achievable, Relevant, and Time-framed. Your financial goals should be inserted in this framework. Make sure your financial goals have a specific dollar amount and a deadline assigned to them. Come up with an example of a goal and lead it through these five aspects.

For example, if you want to take a two-week vacation to Italy to celebrate your anniversary, how would this goal look in SMART terms?

You've looked into dates, flights, accommodations, and concluded that the trip would cost $2000. You want to go next year — in twelve months. This means that you have twelve months to save $2000. This means you have to save $167/month. Do you find saving this amount realistic based on your income? Can you spare this money?

If not, you have to reevaluate the goal, the deadline, or the budget. Whether you start to save earlier, whether you change the destination, it's up to you. If you do find the saving to be realistic for you, great job, you just set a SMART goal!

The goal is specific: a two-week trip to Italy. It is measurable: $2000. If you can save $167 a month, it means the goal is achievable. It is also relevant. You don't have an anniversary every day, after all. Finally, the goal is time-framed — in twelve months.

If you only have $100 extra each month, it is unrealistic to think that, within a year, you'll save $2000. If this is the case, a better goal would be having only a one-week Italy trip, or planning a domestic trip, or simply pledging to save $1000 to have an emergency cushion for the anniversary and just spend quality-time with your spouse in a nearby forest, organizing a picnic, a hike trip –

there are so many meaningful things you can do that don't cost a thing.

101 Budgeting Tips

The first rule of budgeting is to not go over your budget. If you find that your expenses are still more than your revenue, I can share some tips with you so you can grasp the basics of budgeting to stay within your income.

The first tip is to cut back a bit on some of your "luxury expenses." We like to feel special and important, and there's nothing wrong with that, but some things can be too much to fit into the average budget. For example, weekly massages could be cut down to once a month.

Another tip to stay in budget is to stop buying the name brand items at the grocery store. While it may be just a dollar here, fifty cents there, it can add up to a good chunk of money. Try to buy high-quality fresh foods you can cook at home.

If you haven't called around to different companies about your bills lately, you might be overpaying. There are special deals insurance and cell phone companies run constantly, so calling and looking at the different offers, changing your package to a better value one could save you some money. This is the way you can reduce your fixed expenses.

Pay off those credit card bills every month. It can be tempting to keep it there and use your money for other things, but it will just end up hurting you in the end. Stay out of debt by paying them off each month. If you can't commit to doing this, avoid credit cards completely.

For those expenses that aren't fixed, consider carrying around cash so you don't spend over your budget. Switching to cash may seem like a hassle at first, but it can be a great help in the long run.

Taxes are an especially easy way to make sure you stick to your budget. For one, you should make sure that your withholding is correct. If you have too much being withheld, the government is taking money from your paycheck. If you don't have enough being withheld, then you could owe taxes once you file them at year's end. Whenever a life change happens, like a marriage or birth of a child, you should make sure that your tax withholding is still correct.

Also, when you file taxes, there are probably a lot of deductions you are missing out on. Take advantage of the itemized deductions that are available by keeping your receipts and asking an accountant for help. This is especially important if you are an independent contractor, because you don't pay taxes until the end of the year.

If you're looking to put aside some money into a savings account, pay your savings account like a bill. Each month, take the money out of what you earned and put it in that savings account of yours. This is helpful to create an emergency fund in case you stop earning as much money or lose your job. You can ask your employer to send a part of your salary automatically to your savings account. This way you won't feel tempted to shortcut your savings.

When I first created a budget for myself, I was at a loss for what to do. Living in New York is anything but cheap, and I quickly realized that my money was going to run out if I didn't put a budget into place. No longer could I spend my money on every rainbow donut; it was time to get serious about getting my finances in shape.

I started a budget with an itemized list of what I was going to spend each month. You know what I discovered? It was a horrible way to budget! There were so many different items on the list that I was completely lost. Does my coffee go in my food expense, my entertainment expense, my treat yourself expense, or something completely different? If it was up to my own mind, it would have gone to the strictly essentials. I couldn't categorize and prioritize my expenses simply by writing them down.

It's not a good approach to spend and then try to put them into categories, right? It is way better to have set categories with a strict spending cap on them and then start spending, being able to track how much buck is left in each category.

I operated my budget with the following categories:

- Boring Bills;
- Food;
- Entertainment;

- Clothes and make-up; (Sorry if I disappointed you with this.)
- Car stuff;
- Cat;
- Unexpected expenses/savings.

I had a very strict cap on each category. Boring bills were every bill that I had to pay from electricity to my car debt. The food category contained only the essential food I was buying. Whenever I ate out or bought some fancy latte, that consumed my entertainment category. Clothes and make-up are a category I don't think I have to explain. Car stuff is mostly gas and parking tickets. The cat category is all about my baby. However, even for her I have a monthly top. She is not the richest cat on earth but she is surrounded by a lot of love.

The most interesting category is my unexpected expenses/savings category. Optimally, this is The Savings category, where I put twenty percent of my income regardless of how much I make (remember, I'm a freelancer), right after the Boring Bills are paid. But as we know, Murphy never sleeps and I might get a cold, my baby might get sick, the wretched car may get sick... so I need to touch this category and pay the due to the odds of the Unexpected Expenses.

Today I budget a little bit differently, but to understand the gist of that, first I will present where I got the budgeting inspiration from.

The 50/20/30 Method

For those who don't like juggling with so many categories, I can recommend the 50/30/20 method of budgeting.[xlvi] I chose to rename this category the 50/20/30 method. Later you'll see why. It doesn't matter if you are a Hampton's socialite or a suburban mom — this budget can work for you. There are only three different categories, so it is easy to remember them and understand where your money is going. These categories are:

- Essential expenses,
- savings,
- and lifestyle choices. [xlvii]

If you are a regular working person, around fifty percent of your income is going to go toward your essential expenses. This being said, you shouldn't be spending more than fifty percent of your income on essentials. If you do, it means that you're either living too luxuriously, or your essential expenses are not optimized. If you take $3,000 home a month, you should try to spend no more than $1,500 on your rent/mortgage, food, transportation, and bills. Sounds harsh? I know it is. And you don't have to follow or believe what I say. Feel free to disagree. I know $1500 dollars is hardly enough for anything these days and if your are not one of the lucky ones who already owns a flat, rental prices can crawl way above this amount. This is when I say sorry. For a $3000/month income, a $1500 flat is a luxury. Cable television? It's a luxury. Blue Apron? It's a luxury.

You can keep these luxuries if they are the most valuable things you can spend your money on.
But then you need to accept the following consequences:

- you won't be able to save as much;
- you won't be able to spend as much on entertainment or personal things (yes, clothes beyond workout gear, home gear, work gear, and pajamas are not essentials);
- you might be in danger of overindulgence and end up in debt.

If you can fit your essential expenses into fifty percent of your income, you're on board. Keep up the good work and try to further optimize this ratio. I bet you wouldn't mind if you could save a few dollars on bills that you could "invest" in more pleasurable activities.

The next category is savings. Experts recommend this is where twenty percent of your income should be going. This is the category that sets you up for the future. Think of your retirement, your savings accounts, or debt and loan payments, if those are applicable.

Thirty percent of your income thus is going to go to your lifestyle choices. This is the "fun" category, but it also includes things that are important but can't be considered as essentials, like your gym membership and cell phone bill. Snacks and coffee also live in this category. They are not strictly food (thus essentials) unless you live on snacks and coffee. If this is the case, you have bigger issues than your budget. Jokes aside, there's a reason that this is the last category I list.

You shouldn't feel bad for wanting to treat yourself, and there's no reason that this thirty percent cannot be used to give yourself a treat. You worked for it.

But for the sake of your long time well-being, make this category the one from which you pinch out percentages if you need to. For example, in the winter months, your bills may be higher because of the heating, thus your "essentials" would eat up fifty-five or sixty percent of your total income instead of fifty. Take this ten percent from your "lifestyle choices" category instead of you "savings." You'll be grateful for it on the long run.

Now you can understand why I prefer to call the 50/30/20 method the 50/20/30 method. It is an order of spending priorities.

Practical Application of the 50/20/30 Method

The 50/20/30 method is flexible, and it can be used differently for different people. To demonstrate this, I'll compare two different budgets — one for a single woman named Jane, and another for an established couple named Rita and Mike.

Jane has just turned twenty-four and is a recent college graduate. Her first job took her to Dallas. While she has student loans, she is able to make the payment each month, plan for retirement, and pay the bills she needs to. Jane is making $38,000 a year. After taxes, she is making $2,375 because about 25% of her income is going toward paying taxes and her contribution to her retirement 401k.

Essential Expenses:
- Rent: $800
- Car Payment: $70

- Utilities: $70
- Groceries: $220

TOTAL: $1,160

This is 48.8% of her take-home pay, which is right in the 50% area that it should be.

Financial Priorities:
- Student Loan Payment: $200
- Roth IRA Contribution: $210
- Savings Account for Travel: $60

TOTAL: $470

This is 19.8% of her take-home pay, easily fitting into the 20% of financial priorities.

Lifestyle Choices: Jane would have $745 to spend on her fun category, which is 31.4% of her income per month. Due to her student loans and new job, Jane is on a tight budget. However, she still manages to stay within the 50/20/30 budget.

Now, let's look at Rita and Mike's budget. This couple is middle-aged with a child who is a teenager. They are much more established than Jane because they are in their mid-40s and have been working at stable jobs for quite some time.

Their household income is $165,000 a year. After their taxes, Rita and Mike make $9,625 a month. They are in a higher tax bracket, so 30% of their income goes to taxes and to their 401k.

Essential Expenses:
- Mortgage: $1,500
- Car and Insurance: $700
- Gas: $230
- Groceries: $380
- Utilities: $140

TOTAL: $2,950

This is just 30.6% of their monthly income that they bring home, which is far less than the 50% allotted.

Financial Priorities:
- Roth IRA Contributions: $1,155
- 529 Account Contributions: $1,600
- Vacation Fund: $300

TOTAL: $3,055

This is 31.7% of their income that they bring home, which is more than the 20% allotted.

Lifestyle Choices: This leaves them with $3,620 left of their income for their fun category. This is 37.6% of their income that they bring home each month.

Rita and Mike's income and situation shows that the 50/20/30 method is fairly flexible. Because they are not on the same budget Jane was, they could allocate more to financial contributions since they were only living on 30% of their income for their essentials. They are saving on their essential expenses so they can save for a college fund for their teenager. Since they are living on less, they can save for retirement.

An important aspect to recognize is that the 50/20/30 method only applies to the income you bring home. Anything you put into your retirement or a health savings account before you get your check is not factored into income. If you are contributing to an account before you get your check, you're probably putting away more money in the savings category than normal, which is a good thing! However, if you are self-employed, retirement should be of the utmost importance to you. It would be beneficial to cut down on some of your fun or essential categories to really max out and save up for retirement.

Everyone has different incomes, values, and priorities, thus your budgeting should never be compared to someone else's. One person may spend $800 on rent while another spends $2,000. Comparing your budget with someone else's will only make you frustrated.

There's no "normal" way to spend your money. You may have to purchase an expensive winter coat because it dips below zero during winter, and someone else may only have to buy tank tops because they live in San Diego year-round. There are a lot of things that aren't in your control, like your zip code, tax bracket, and/or the weather of where you live, so you should really just be trying to find your "normal."

Defining "normal" isn't as hard as you fear it may be. Your needs should be limited to 50%, your savings to at least 20%, and your wants limited to 30%. It is straightforward at first, but it is going to require you to track your money like a hawk for a bit. Ask yourself these three questions to help yourself set a budget that works for you:

- *Can I make my habits work for me, instead of me working for my habits?*

- *Am I spending every dollar I earn on something I could be saving my energy or time on?*

- *What options can help me to become financially stable? (Not everyone can afford mortgages and car payments.)*

The best part of this budget system is that the percentages make things easy. If your income drops, the percentages give you a clear way on how to much money can you spend in each category, and if your income rises, you can adjust the percentages to save more or whatever else you want.

The important thing is to not hesitate. Get out a piece of paper and calculate your budget with these percentages. This can show you whether or not your budgeting is lining up how it should. For example, if your budget looks something like this:

Essentials: 70%

Savings: 0%

Lifestyle choice: 30%

Something is clearly wrong with this budget. If your expenses look like that, it is time to change it up a bit. Look into your essentials and lifestyle choices and see how you could reduce them. Your savings are very important, so they should be treated as such. Also remember that the 30% of your income you are putting toward lifestyle choices is last on the list. That category should be 0% before your savings are at 0.

My Budgeting Method Today

Not too long ago, I was struggling with my budget. Believe it or not, I'm not a millionaire who is writing all my wisdom down to share. Quite honestly, listening to financial advice from millionaires is the worst because they simply cannot connect to those who are struggling to stay afloat financially. It's a whole different world, and while there is nothing wrong with that, know that I'm writing this book to help the average Joe.

I'm a freelance web designer and writer who lives in New York. I design and do creative work in New York. I already know what you're thinking, and it's true! It is a hard industry to be in when you live in New York, and the big city's prices are nowhere near affordable. I'm 32 years old, and I make about $1,700 a month after taxes, putting money in savings, paying my insurances, and contributing to my retirement.

The good news is that I don't have any rent. I own my flat, thanks to my parents, but I still pay utilities of about $200 a month. On top of that, my car lease is $330, I pay $100 in pet costs each month, my phone is $50, and my streaming services are $20 a month. Usually, I pay everything on my credit card, which amounts to another $1,000 a month, but I make sure to pay it off every month.

Because I do freelance work, I never know for sure just how much money I am going to bring home each month. However, those above numbers are my average (with a little alteration to protect my unimportant privacy). I use these modified estimates to illustrate my own budget.

In any case, I'm not your millionaire or billionaire living in New York. In fact, I'm far from it. Before you think I may not have a leg to stand on when it comes to talking about finances, let me convince you why I *do.*

I'm not the type of person who is trying to get rich or die trying. I'm just your average girl with a baby cat (don't worry, I only have one. I'm not a crazy cat lady… yet) and I live in New York, trying to make ends meet. However, my life hasn't always been sunshine and daisies. I found myself at the end of an important relationship a few years back, so I took my heartbreak and went around the world to do some traveling. This lasted two years, and when I came back, I knew it was time to change. To grow up if you like.

I've had some bad spending habits in the past. I have been in debt. My financial situation has been far more dire than it is today, but I have turned it around. Here I am, talking about finances so I can help others change the way their finances are working for them. I've paid off almost all of my debt, besides my Lamborghini.

Did I get you with that one? As cool as a Lamborghini would be to drive, I actually drive a very non-fancy Toyota Camry. Jealous yet?

In all seriousness, being in debt and worrying about your finances is no fun, and I have been there with you. Thankfully, my income is increasing as the months go on, and I'm excited to grow it so that I can budget within the 50/20/30 method.

Instead of writing down all of my budgeting stuff on paper, I decided to go with the app Mint.com. I love that I can access my budget right on my phone, and saving paper is always a plus! Papers can end up cluttering up your place, and it is bad for the environment.

Mint.com is a totally free finance app that can help you budget. It doesn't discriminate based on whether you have an iPhone or an Android. If you've tried Mint and it isn't for you, there's another great app that is called youneedabudget.com. While this app is really awesome, it does cost $4.17 a month, so it is something to think about.

Another reason apps are useful is that many of them will connect straight to your bank account so that your budget is always up to date. No longer do you have to pull out a pen and piece of paper to write down every time you purchase something. However, inputting your expenses like you do in the app is a great way to help you realize where your money is going. It is like a tap on the shoulder telling you about the money you just spent. It makes you aware of everything coming in and out of your account. The apps can also help to group your purchases into categories, but this isn't always accurate.

The first month you budget, I recommend you keep a journal and write down all your expenses and categorize them yourself. This helps you realize how much money you are spending in the large and small categories. Don't forget about these small purchases just because they don't seem to matter. They are still important and can affect your budgeting.

While you can never predict a car accident, I have found over the years that many unexpected costs can usually be expected. Perhaps you are driving on practically bald tires, but then you're shocked when one of them blows out and you have to replace it. The same goes for things like buying holiday gifts for your children's teacher. You do this *every* year, so it really isn't some unexpected cost. In actuality, you should set aside a small amount of money each month that helps you save up for these "unexpected" costs.

Percentage Spreadsheet

If you want an estimate of everything you spend your money on, there's an online spreadsheet put together by themesquitegroup.org that has different percentages of how you should spend your money. If you're not thrilled with the 50/20/30 method, I highly recommend you try out this one. The categories go like this:

Housing — Suggested percentage is 30%
Total Housing Costs / Net Monthly Income = your housing percentage

Transportation — Suggested percentage is 15%

Total Transportation Costs / Net Monthly Income = your transportation percentage

Food & Household — Suggested percentage is 15%

Total Food & Household Costs / Net Monthly Income = your food & household percentage

Savings — Suggested percentage is 10% or more

Total Savings Costs / Net Monthly Income = your savings percentage

Debt — Suggested percentage is 15% or less

Total Debt Costs / Net Monthly Income = your debt percentage

Miscellaneous — Suggested percentage is 15%

Total Miscellaneous Costs / Net Monthly Income = your miscellaneous percentage [xlviii]

Paying attention to these suggested percentages is very important to keeping with this budgeting system. If you find that you are over the percentage in any of these categories, you have to find ways to cut costs. For example, living somewhere that costs more than 30% of your income doesn't work with this budgeting system, so you would need to save by getting a cheaper place to stay. This could mean finding a smaller apartment, or even moving to another state. The housing markets can be crazy in some of the more popular East Coast and West Coast states, but the rate of income doesn't change that much from state to state. You could be living the same quality of life, or better, just by moving somewhere else.

This budgeting system works as long as you stick to it.

Housing Questions

Even if you've cut costs, you might think that your housing cost is one that will always plague you. In decades past, the way to a good life was to have a stable job, a nice spouse, 3.5 kids, and a mortgage payment. Times have changed. People are getting married later or choosing not to marry at all, having fewer kids, and housing costs have risen. Millennials find themselves in a disastrous situation when it comes to trying to find a house they can afford.

For most of us, we are confused and lost when it comes to housing costs. Is it better to rent? To own? To live out in the middle of the sea where you don't need to worry about anything but storms and fishing?

If you're wondering how much you should be spending on your housing each month, you are not alone. Thankfully, there are experts who have shed some light on this issue. Most of them recommend that you spend about 30% of your income on your rent or mortgage each month. This is calculated based on your gross monthly income before taxes are taken out. Just divide your yearly income by 40 to get the number you should be spending per month on a house.[xlix]

This rule doesn't apply to everyone. For those who have debt, like student loans, those should be factored into whatever it is that you are paying. If you don't have any debts, the 30% rule may work perfectly for you.

Since many of us have debts, let me introduce you to the 43% rule. The new and improved percentage rule, the 43% rule says that your housing payment *and* your monthly debts shouldn't go above 43% of your monthly income. Those who have high debt payments may feel like they won't have enough money left over for their rent or mortgage. These are serious concerns, but there are ways to help you with that. Many companies will help refinance your student loans for a lower rate so that you could still pay monthly toward them, but you would have more money to spend on rent. [1]

Sometimes, you can't control how much your rent is going to be. Those who live in a rural area may only pay around $800 a month for an apartment, but those who live in the expensive metropolitan areas, like Los Angeles, New York, Boston, and Washington, D.C., are going to be looking at over $1,500 for a small one bedroom or studio-sized apartment. In those cases, your 30-43% isn't going to stretch very far. There are probably going to be some sacrifices on your end that need to be made.

When looking at the rental listings, factor in the cost of utilities. If that is already included in the rent, a slightly higher rent per month would be worth it. However, if they are not factored into the rent, then you'll probably need to look at a smaller budget.

There are ways you can save money even if you live in a big city. For instance, you could sell your car and save on gas by taking public transportation, if your apartment is close enough to your workplace. You can consciously choose an apartment close to your workplace. Still, you need to accept that you might need to cut back on eating out, cable, and going on vacations until your income is steadier and you can afford to do these things.

If you're single, a roommate may be a good option to save some bucks on housing. Splitting the cost of a two-bedroom apartment is much cheaper than paying for a one-bedroom by yourself.

For those who are looking into buying a home, it can be just as stressful, if not more, than finding a place to rent. When you purchase a home, you're stuck with it, so you want to make sure it is something that you can comfortably afford. A great online resource that I have found is: http://www.bankrate.com/calculators/mortgages/new-house-calculator.aspx. This is an online calculator where you put in everything from your income to your car payment, and it tells you how much you can comfortably afford when you purchase a new home. No one wants to feel overwhelmed after they buy a home because they can't afford it, so this gives you an idea of whether or not you should jump the gun.

Chapter 5: How Did I Get Out of Debt?

I won't make a mind-blowing statement when I say that the United States is a nation largely run on debt. It can still be surprising though to learn about the most recent charts on how big this debt is and how it can be broken down to individual "contributions."

According to recent data from Comet, this is the reality of Americans having debt today:

- 80.9% of Baby Boomers,
- 79.9% of Gen Xers,
- 81.5% of Millennials.[li]

The leading type of debt is credit card debt, closely followed by student loans, mortgages, vehicle debt, and medical debt. The charts of Comet also showed that medical debt is the number one cause of personal bankruptcy in the US.

If you're struggling with debt, having a hard time keeping up with your payments, it's crucial to take steps to address the problem. I know firsthand how hard it is to be in debt. There are some days where you feel like you're just drowning in it and won't ever break the surface. Today I can say I'm finally (almost) debt free. This didn't happen overnight though, didn't happen effortlessly, and not without a great virtual mentor. I used Dave Ramsey's 7 Baby Steps technique. [lii]

As the name suggests, there are seven things you need to do to get yourself out of debt. When I was struggling with my student loan and traveling debt, these seven steps seemed nearly impossible.

Thankfully, I persevered and can now preach about how amazing these steps are.

Step One — Save $1,000 [liii]

If you have debt, there's a good chance that you don't have much or any savings. Dave Ramsey strongly recommends having an emergency fund, no matter how far into debt you are. This fund can be used for things like a blown-out tire, a medical expense that was unexpected, or to live off of if you lose your job. While $1,000 isn't a lot of money, it is still a lot better than nothing.

Saving $1,000 for me was a big challenge. I do freelance work and write books, I don't have that steady trickle of income coming in I can securely count on. Thus the $1,000 in savings just didn't seem practical. However, after reading all of Dave Ramsey's seven steps, I knew I had to make an effort.

Since my normal income wasn't going to cut it, I decided to save $1,000 by putting everything I made from my first book into savings. That money didn't come in overnight, so it took a little while for me to save up the $1,000. However, once it was finally saved, it felt amazing!

Step Two — Pay Off Your Debt [liv]

This might just be the most important step in the seven steps. To get out of debt, I knew that I was going to need to make some changes. When I looked over at my student loan bills, I was discouraged. You pay a few hundred dollars a month for these loan payments, yet it seems like the total amount you owe never gets smaller.

I used what Dave Ramsey calls the snowball method to pay off my debts. Right now, I only have my car payment as a debt, but I still pay that off with as much money as I can per month. If you have multiple debts, the snowball method is perfect for you.

Imagine a snowball rolling down a snowy mountain. What does it do as it rolls? The snowball gets bigger. And bigger. And bigger! Soon enough, there's a building-sized ball of snow that has come to a stop at the edge of the mountain. You are going to pay off your debt just like this rolling snowball.

To start paying off your debt, you first need to line them all up. List all of your debts and prioritize paying off the highest interest ones first.

Then figure out how much you can pay toward your other debts each month. Make the minimum payment on every debt that you have. Just remember to carve out some of your income and put a bigger payment on the debt with the highest interest.

For example, let's say you have a $300 credit card bill, a $5,000 student loan, and a $10,000 car payment. Your credit card bill has a 25% interest rate, your student loan has a 5% interest rate, and your car payment has a 4% interest rate. You pay the $25 per month minimum for your credit card, the $130 minimum on your student loan, and the $200 minimum on your car loan. That's a total of $355 you pay per month on your debts.

However, you should carve out your income and see where you can add some more money to your credit card payment, since that one is continually growing. If you add $50 to your credit card per month, you are going to pay that off faster than if you stuck with the $25 minimum payment that was due.

If you manage to pay $75 a month toward your credit card, in a few months, your credit card is paid off completely. Now you have $75 extra a month to put toward your student loan payment. You're building your snowball to make your debt smaller. Now instead of $130 per month, you're paying $205 per month on your student loan payment. Once your student loan payment is paid off, roll that money into your car loan so that you're paying $405 per month for your car instead of the $200 you were paying before.

Soon enough, all of your debts will be paid off! This method made it easy for me to pay off my student loans. Now that my student loans are paid off, I roll that payment into my car payment every month.

Step Three — Full Emergency Fund [lv]

If you've followed Dave Ramsey's baby steps, you already have the $1,000 in your savings account. However, the $1000 emergency fund is just the beginning. Ramsey strongly advises that you have three to six months of your expenses in your savings account. I recommend this too. Let me tell you why.

At any given time, something could happen that would make you lose your income completely. Whether you are laid off from your job or in an accident, these events usually happen when you're unprepared. If you don't have an emergency fund, that adds stress during your job search or recovery. A sizable emergency fund could make your life a little less stressful.

When you pay off your debt with the snowball method, you still have a lump sum of money that you're used to paying toward your debts. Think of this as your next snowball and put everything you were paying toward your debts into an emergency fund. Continue saving until you have at least three months of your income saved.

Step Four — Invest 15% ^{lvi}

The scary "I" word. If you would have muttered the word "invest" to me a few years ago, I would have run for the hills. Investing is scary. You think of all the bad calls people make in the stock market and how they go from millions to bankrupt overnight. The good news is, you really don't have to worry about such an extreme outcome. You don't have to get into the stock market at all if you don't want to.

Investing is important to your future, no matter how scared of it you might be. Unless you want to be working until the day you die, you have to start thinking about retirement. It doesn't matter if you're eighteen or fifty.

By the time you don't have any debts to pay and you have an emergency fund to cushion you if you fall, investing fifteen percent of your income should be nothing! Try to invest in a 401(k) and Roth IRA. Lots of companies have plans that will match whatever contributions you put into your 401(k). However, if your company does not offer matching your contributions, or you own your own business, go straight to putting your money into a Roth IRA. It will work better for what you need it for. If you don't know what 401(k) and Roth IRA is, learn more about them here: https://www.bankrate.com/investing/ira/roth-ira-401k-whats-the-difference/.

Meeting with a financial advisor and talking about investments is a great idea. They can find out more about which investments will work best for your income in the long run.

Step Five — College Plan [lvii]

This is my favorite step in Dave Ramsey's plan. I'm joking since I don't have children. As much as

I would like to think that my fur baby is smart enough to go to cat college, it isn't really something I need to save for – yet.

I can advise you, the parent, from the other side of having student loans. I know the hardship of paying off student loans right after you fly out of college, thus I recommend you, as a parent, to try to save for your children's college education. I'm sure you don't want your children not attending university because they cannot afford it, or entering in debt at the real start of their lives. Even if your children are young, saving up for college is never something that is done too early. The amount American colleges charge for even just one semester is mind-blowing.

There are two different funds that are good for saving for college educations. There is the 529 college savings fund and the ESA or Educations Savings Account. Both of these are ways to save for your child's education with advantages on your taxes. These investment funds are split amongst the four different types of mutual funds like your retirement account. A lot of this will vary depending on how much you make and what state you live in.

Step Six — Pay Off Your Home[lviii]

Imagine yourself without a mortgage. That is a fantasy that could be your reality.

If you don't have any debt except a mortgage, it is time to snowball that huge amount you have been putting into savings and pay off your home. Most people can pay off their home within 10 years, if they follow the Dave Ramsey method. For those with a 30-year mortgage, consider switching it to a 15-year mortgage and refinance. This can save you a lot of interest and it helps to keep your goal of paying off your home early at the forefront of your mind.

Step Seven — Build Wealth and Give [lix]

You know the saying that it is much better to give than it is to receive? Well, that saying is true, friends! When you're completely debt-free, it feels wonderful to live your life. This is not some alternate universe or unreachable goal. No matter what your finances are like right now, wealth can be in the palm of your hand in just a few years. The key to this step is not to give away all you have. Building your wealth for your future generations is important, but you still want to make the world a better place.

If you couldn't tell already, I am passionate about my cat. I think cats are amazing, independent creatures, and I like to donate to my favorite no-kill shelter here in New York City. This is a cause

I feel good about, and a small donation from me can go a long way at the shelter. You don't have to have thousands of dollars to give to make a difference. Even a small amount can help others. Remember this when you start to give to other foundations.

I truly appreciate the knowledge and work of Mr. Ramsey. Reading his work helped me to improve financially. To learn more about Dave Ramsey's work you can check out his website, www.daveramsey.com, or his book, Total Money Makeover.

Chapter 6: Long-Term Lifestyle Changes

Keeping things simple is one of my mottos, and I like to apply this to both my finances and the way I live my life. Thankfully, those two things usually go hand in hand.

When you keep things simple, you are spending mindfully within your budget. Spending less than you make seems like the simplest thing in the world, but it isn't. We have an average of four different credit cards in our wallets, and many people don't pay them off every month. Even though you can tell a person over and over again to spend less than they make, it doesn't seem to matter. The problem continues, and it is a never-ending cycle.

I can tell you that you should spend less money than you make once again, but it won't affect you unless you decide to commit to a change. You'll never get out of debt if you continue to spend more money than you make. Recognize how much money you really need to survive; it's almost shockingly little. Then take your wants under a microscope. What you want is rarely what you *need*.

Declutter Your Finances

Just like you clean up and organize rooms that become too messy to live in, you should look at your finances every few months and do a financial clean up on them as well. Cleaning and decluttering your finances can help you simplify your financial life and make it easier to keep track of everything.

Start with cleaning up your checking and savings accounts. You should have one of each of these. Use your checking account to pay all of your bills, and your savings account to hold your emergency fund and future goals in a safe place.

After you've cleaned up these two, look through your wallet. If you can name all the major credit card brands by looking at the slots in your wallet, it is time to get rid of most of them. Decide on *one* credit card to use. Yes, just one.

Take advantage of the automation that comes nowadays with your bank accounts. Setting up autopay for your bills, investments, savings, and credit payments makes it easy so that you never have to remember to pay things when they are due! This can help you avoid late fees that come with forgetting to pay things.

Do a clean-up of your email address. If you think that your email doesn't have a thing to do with your finances, you couldn't be more wrong. Right now, you're probably signed up for different subscriptions and each day, you get an email claiming that there is 50% off online at your favorite store, or free shipping at a place that *never* does free shipping. You get bombarded with ads and marketing campaigns by the hour, and they convince you to shop.

Do yourself a favor and go through your email and unsubscribe from all of these stores. While you won't get as many coupons, it will make things easier when you're trying to manage your money.

Breaking the Money Bond

Some people are slaves to their money. They think their worth rests in how much money they make. Don't buy into this nonsense. You are an amazing person regardless if you make a million dollars a year or a few thousand dollars a year. Your worth doesn't depend on the money that you make. We all have to survive, and it takes money to do that, but decide why you might want to give up on money being the primary focus in your life.

I don't make millions of dollars, but I do use the money I have to live minimally while still living meaningfully. I love the freedom that comes with my approach to money. It can be easy to get wrapped up in them, but taking a step back and questioning the purchases you make can help bring you back down to earth.

Over the years, with the many different experiences around the world that I've had, I realize that the best things in life don't cost anything. The solutions to the many problems that we experience are right in the palm of our hands. They include having more gratitude, lowering our expectations, and living with a bit more heart.

Challenge 33 [lx]

Challenge 33 is a project many people are trying out. What it entails is you live with just thirty-three items of clothing and try it out for three months. This may sound daunting, but it's a challenge that lots of people are doing, and they *love* it. According to Bemorewithless.com, Challenge 33 started out with the desire to dress with less.

If you're looking to do this challenge, all you need to do is choose thirty-three items of clothing. This clothing encompasses your daily clothing, your shoes, accessories, jewelry, and outerwear. However, workout clothing, your sentimental jewelry that you never take off, sleepwear, underwear, and loungewear is not included in your thirty-three items of clothing.

To start, look through all the clothes that you have and get rid of anything that is broken or too threadbare to be frequently worn for the next three months. Then choose your thirty-three items of clothing. Remember, you have to live in them for three months, so choose items that are practical. You don't want ten pairs of pants, three shirts, fifteen pieces of jewelry, and five pairs of shoes. Instead, you should have a good variety of shirts, a few pairs of pants, a few pieces of jewelry that you can pair with different outfits, and a few pairs of shoes.

After you have picked out your thirty-three items, box up everything else and seal it shut. Take it to your parents' house, your storage unit, or put it high up in the garage. This box (or boxes) is not to be touched for the next ninety days!

Once the challenge is over, I bet you'll find that you love it. While you might want to bring back an item or two of clothing, remember how great it felt to have that much space and time to yourself? There was no endless worrying about what to wear like you may have done before. Simplifying your wardrobe seems to make things so much easier.

Bring the box of your old clothes down and donate anything that you aren't going to wear. You could always swap out an item from your current thirty-three clothing pieces with a different item from your box. You'll need different wardrobe pieces for summer and winter, so keep that in mind when you're going through and donating your clothes.

This challenge should bring you happiness, so don't suffer through it. If you find your clothes don't fit well or they aren't in the best shape, there's no reason to keep them around any longer. However, you'll find that with less clothing, you experience less of a desire to shop than you did before! It's a great way to start, or continue, your minimalism journey. It saves you time, and it also saves you money. Isn't that something we could all live with a little more of?

Hygge

If you're unfamiliar with the concept of *hygge*, let me introduce you to one of the best-kept cozy secrets. Hygge comes straight from Denmark. People around the world are doing it for the joy that it brings. It is simple, inexpensive, and makes life better.

This funny-looking word is pronounced "hoogah." It rolls off the tongue! Fun, right? Hygge is about bringing the coziness of life into your day by getting joy from the little things. You know when you are outside in the snow and you come indoors to a crackling fireplace? There really isn't anything better than the warm fire soothing the coolness from your hands.

Show gratitude every day for the life that you live and find balance in how you are living your life. It isn't about living clean, or anything like that. In fact, hygge actually encourages you to indulge yourself and stop the restriction that is so popular in our culture these days! I mean, if something is telling me that I can eat that extra peppermint truffle that I love so much, who am *I* to argue with *it*?

If you don't know how to incorporate hygge into your life, have no fear. I've put together a little list with simple ways to live your best life with some hygge on the side.[lxi]

Have a Bake-Off

Hygge is about indulging yourself, and there's nothing better than a homemade treat. You know that amazing muffin recipe that you only make for special occasions? Indulge yourself just this once and make that cake. Having a bake-off can relieve stress and make you feel better. Plus, the warmth of the oven and the sweet scent of freshly baked goods heats up your home for an ultra-cozy feel.

Cost: You can bake your own blueberry muffins for as little as $0.95 per piece.[lxii] Of course, when you buy all the ingredients, this price will be higher.

Read a Book

Remember the days when you used to curl up in your soft blanket with a good book? Now that things are so busy, you might feel like you've forgotten how to read. Look up some recommendations online and read one of the many books you have missed out on over the years. You won't regret it!

Cost: A good book can cost as much as $0! Check book promotion sites like Book Bub or Buck Books to find some good deals.

Buy Something Cozy

I've got two words for you: Fuzzy. Socks. There is nothing better than having a warm pair of fluffy socks. I am convinced that the fuzziness of socks can cure most of the things that are wrong in the world.

Cost: You can buy a pair of cozy socks in Daiso for $1.5 or a dollar store for just a buck.

Drink a Hot Toddy

Are you a latte lover? A hot toddy person? Tea? Hot cocoa? Literally all of those things are great options. Hot drinks have the ability to make us all feel a bit better. The warmth and steam rising up from the cup to hit our nostrils makes everything feel good again. Try to be mindful while drinking your cocoa. First indulge your other senses, not your taste buds. Bring your nose close to the cup and inhale the sweet chocolate scent of your drink. How does it feel? Open your eyes and immerse in the view of the lovely creaminess. Try to listen as the small air bubbles pop on the top of your cocoa. Breathe in to your palms, feel the delicate warmth of your cup. Then slowly move the cup close to your mouth and taste the sweet drink. Before swallowing it, take note of the taste you sense, the texture that touches your tongue. Now slowly, allow it to warm you up.

Cost: One gallon of milk costs $3.99 – $4.99 on average. One pound of raw cocoa powder costs around $9. One gallon of milk however is enough for sixteen cups of cocoa. One pound of raw cocoa powder is enough for even more cups of cocoa. Thus, if we only calculate with sixteen cups for the $14 cost, it's still $0.88 per cup.

Slow Cook Your Meal

You don't have to throw Gatsby-style dinner parties to celebrate hygge. In fact, the easier the dinner, the better. Slow cooking your meal is a great way to get a healthy meal and have a fragrant and delicious dish to eat.

Cost: Depends on the meal. According to research, the average home made meal costs $4-5 while restaurant meals hardly ever cost less than $13.[lxiii]

Give Yourself a Spa Day

Indulging in a self-made spa day is perfect to make yourself feel a little cozier. Taking time for yourself is important. Treat your skin to some pampering and paint your nails.

Cost: I can only come up with Daiso, again. You can get their bulk face mask deal (five masks per package) for $1.5. For the same price you can buy other self-pampering tools like nail polish, soap, bathing sponge.

Write a Letter

Writing is already soothing, but mix that with some love and gratitude you have in your life. Everyone likes receiving an old fashioned, hand-written letter, so try writing a letter to a loved one.

Cost: Currently at USPS a letter stamp costs $0.50.[lxiv]

Light Candles

Turning down artificial lights and lighting some candles can help you appreciate a long winter, a tired evening, a difficult life period. Doing your chores by candlelight makes everything seem a bit better, and it certainly enhances the mood of drinking your hot cocoa. If you want to add an extra touch to this practice, choose scented candles.

Cost: You can buy candles starting from $1 at a Dollar Store.

Write or Draw

Harness your creative energy and write or draw something just for the sake of art. This can be a poem, a short story, a pencil sketch or a painting. Start a journal and write down some of your happiest memories and illustrate them. Feel free to create whatever it is that comes to your mind. It's your personal artistic haven.

Cost: You can buy a 500 –piece A4 paper pack for less than $8 on amazon. Yes, that's 500 drawings. You can get pencils for free from different companies who are happy to give them to you. It's free advertising for them.

Watch a Sappy Movie

Oh, yes, I'm talking about a major tear-jerking movie here. You know that movie you never watch because it makes you cry, but you love it so much? Well, do it! Watching this sappy movie might make you cry, but you'll love it.

Cost: It can be as little as $0.

Show Your Love

A great way to practice hygge is to show your love to the world. Share your gratitude by inviting over friends and socializing with them. If your friends are far away, take some time to call them and see how they are doing. Do you like social media? Share a video about someone who did something heartwarming to other people. I love watching these videos in my Facebook feed. Regardless if the video is a set up or a real story, seeing goodness in the world makes my heart hopeful and filled with love.

Cost: Love don't cost a thing.

Take a Bath

Take a long, hot bath; with bubbles, duckling and all. If you have a small amount of money left in your "lifestyle choices" budget category, buy some Epsom salts or a bath bomb. Just a few dollars can get you many baths with Epsom salts, and you'll feel like a million dollars.

Cost: It can be free (or rather as much as a bathtub-worth of water costs), you can buy bath foam in a Dollar Store for $1. Epsom Salt costs $8.99 for a two-pound size on Amazon. If you want to make a real bargain deal, get the nineteen-pound version for $27. It might be a big one-time purchase, but that will be enough for more than forty baths. Again, less than a dollar for the lovely experience.

Create Season-Based Home Decoration

What season is now? Right now, when I'm writing this book, it's fall. Oh, I love fall. So many opportunities there to create lovely decoration for your home. From fallen leaves to chestnuts and walnuts, you can create so many pretty, creative things for your dinner table, window sill, or shelves. Separate one hour each Sunday to prepare some seasonal decorations. If you have kids, they will love this task. If you live alone, you'll be thrilled to have a tiny creative corner once in a while. In the summer and spring, you can use flowers or flowery branches for decoration. In the winter, you need to put in some extra skill – learn to knit for instance and make a scarf and hat for your favorite teddy bear.

Cost: If you are creative, it can cost you nothing. Just collect whatever you can find in nature.

Make it a habit to pamper yourself with low-cost activities. On one hand, experience simply gives so much more nourishment to the soul than physical things, on the other hand, becoming more of a minimalist can help you with the three major problems discussed in this book: compulsive shopping and overspending, hoarding, and financial difficulties.

The great thing about minimalism is, you don't need to "cure" yourself out of your addictions, just lead them in a different direction. You need to shop? Buy something purposefully cheap but heartwarming – like a candle, or baking ingredients. Do you feel the need to hoard? Collect lovely, self-made decorations. The majority of the tips I provided above cost less than a dollar. However, they can bring joy and fulfillment in your life, distracting you from the vicious spending and shopping tendencies.

Depending on the seriousness of your shopping, hoarding, and spending addiction, my advice on budgeting and life-style change might be enough. In any case, this book doesn't replace the face-to-face diagnosis of a specialist. I strongly recommend you to go, visit one just to make sure you don't need any additional treatment to some good ol' self-help books like this one.

If you do need additional treatment, follow it with faith. You can still use my tips to enrich your life regardless of what your specialist prescribed you. A good book, a cup of cocoa, or some creative self-expression never hurt anybody.

I wish you good luck with your progress!

Best,

Mitch

Reference

Addicion.com. Shopping Addiction. Addiction.com. 2018. https://www.addiction.com/addiction-a-to-z/shopping-addiction/

American Psychiatric Association. *Hoarding Disorder*. American Psychiatric Association. 2013.

American Psychological Association. American Psychological Association Survey Shows Money Stress Weighing on Americans' Health Nationwide. American Psychological Association. 2015. http://www.apa.org/news/press/releases/2015/02/money-stress.aspx

Berger, Vincent. Dr. *Spending and Shopping Addiction*. Psychologist Anywhere Anytime.

2005.
http://www.psychologistanywhereanytime.com/ad
diction_psychologist/psychologist_addiction_spen
ding.htm

Better Help. What Is Axis II Personality Disorder?
Better   Help.   2018.
https://www.betterhelp.com/advice/personality-
disorders/what-is-axis-ii-personality-disorder/

Black, Donald W., Martha Shaw, and Nancee
Blum. "Pathological Gambling and Compulsive
Buying: Do They Fall within an Obsessive-
Compulsive Spectrum?" Dialogues in Clinical
Neuroscience 12.2 175–185. Print. (2010)

Bratiotis, Christiana, PhD. Otte, Suzanne, MSW.
Steketee, Gail, PhD. Muroff, Jordana, PhD. Frost,
Randy O. PhD. *What is compulsive hoarding?*
International   OCD   Foundation.   2009.

https://iocdf.org/wp-content/uploads/2014/10/Hoarding-Fact-Sheet.pdf

Brewer, Judson A., Marc N. Potenza. The Neurobiology and Genetics of Impulse Control Disorders: Relationships to Drug Addictions. Biochemical pharmacology 75.1 (2008): 63–75. PMC. Web. 12 Sept. 2018.

Canning, Kristin. 6 Ways to Practice Hygge, the Danish Secret to Happiness. Health. 2017. https://www.health.com/mind-body/hygge

Clinic, Mayo. Hoarding Disorder. Mayo Clinic. 2017. https://www.mayoclinic.org/diseases-conditions/hoarding-disorder/diagnosis-treatment/drc-20356062

Christenson GA. Faber JR. de Zwann M. Compulsive buying: descriptive characteristics and psychiatric comorbidity. J Clin Psychiatry. 1994; 55:5–11.

Comet. The Details of Debt. Comet. 2018. https://www.cometfi.com/details-of-debt

Cruz, Veronica. *Impulse spending reduced if you get organized.* Market Business News. 2014. https://marketbusinessnews.com/impulse-spending-reduced-get-organized/12030

Frank, Hannah & Stewart, Elyse & Walther, Michael & Benito, Kristen & Freeman, Jennifer & Conelea, Christine & Garcia, Abbe. (2013). Hoarding behavior among young children with obsessive–compulsive disorder. Journal of Obsessive-Compulsive and Related Disorders. 3. 10.1016/j.jocrd.2013.11.001.

Howard Rosenthal, Human Services Dictionary p. 102. 2003.

Jantz, Gregory L. Ph.D. *The Psychology Behind Hoarding.* Psychology Today. 2014. https://www.psychologytoday.com/blog/hope-relationships/201409/the-psychology-behind-hoarding

Illiades, Chris. Md. *How I stopped compulsive shopping.* Everyday Health. 2013. https://www.everydayhealth.com/depression/how-i-stopped-compulsive-shopping.aspx

Investopedia. *Compulsive Shopping.* Investopedia. 2017.
https://www.investopedia.com/terms/c/compulsive-shopping.asp

Klontz, Brad. Do You Have a Money Disorder? Psychology Today. 2010. https://www.psychologytoday.com/us/blog/mind-over-money/201001/do-you-have-money-disorder

Klotz, Brad. Mind Over Money. Crown Business. 2009.

Lendkey. *How Much of Your Income Should You Spend on Housing?* Lend Key. 2015. https://www.lendkey.com/blog/how-much-of-your-income-should-you-spend-on-housing/

Miltenberger RG. Redlin J. Crosby R, et al. Direct and retrospective assessment of factors contributing to compulsive buying. J Behav Ther Exp Psychiatry. 2003;34:1–9.

Mint. *The 50/20/30 Rule for Minimalist Budgeting.* Mint Life. 2016. https://blog.mint.com/saving/the-minimalist-guide-to-budgeting-in-your-20s-072016/

My Money Coach. *What is Budgeting? What is a Budget?* My Money Coach. 2017. https://www.mymoneycoach.ca/budgeting/what-is-a-budget-planning-forecasting

Njeri Gitimu, Priscilla. Gitmu Waithaka, Abel. *Retail Therapy: Its relationship to Gender, Life Engagement, and Subjective Happiness (PDF).* Youngstown State University. 2017. http://www.documentshare.org/health-and-fitness/retail-therapy-its-relationship-to-gender-life-engagement-and-subjective-happiness/

Pertusa A., Frost R.O., Fullana M. A., Samuels J., Steketee G., Tolin D., Saxena S., Leckman J.F., Mataix-Cols D. *Refining the boundaries of compulsive hoarding: A review.* Clinical Psychology Review. 30: 371–386. 2010.

Pertusa, Alberto M.D. Fullana Miguel A., Ph.D. Singh, Satwant M.Sc. Alonso, Pino M.D., Ph.D. Menchón, José M. M.D., Ph.D. Mataix-Cols David, Ph.D Compulsive Hoarding: OCD Symptom, Distinct Clinical Syndrome, or Both? Psychiatry Online. 2008. https://ajp.psychiatryonline.org/doi/pdfplus/10.117 6/appi.ajp.2008.07111730

Psychguides. Shopping Addiction Symptoms, Causes and Effects. Psychguides. 2018. https://www.psychguides.com/guides/shopping-addiction-symptoms-causes-and-effects/

Ramsey, Dave. *Dave Ramsey's 7 Baby Steps.* Dave Ramsey. 2017. https://www.daveramsey.com/baby-steps

Ramsey, Dave. *Baby Step 1.* Dave Ramsey. 2017. https://www.daveramsey.com/baby-steps/1

Ramsey, Dave. *Baby Step 2.* Dave Ramsey. 2017. https://www.daveramsey.com/baby-steps/2

Ramsey, Dave. *Baby Step 3.* Dave Ramsey. 2017. https://www.daveramsey.com/baby-steps/3

Ramsey, Dave. *Baby Step 4.* Dave Ramsey. 2017. https://www.daveramsey.com/baby-steps/4

Ramsey, Dave. *Baby Step 5.* Dave Ramsey. 2017 https://www.daveramsey.com/baby-steps/5

Ramsey, Dave. *Baby Step 6.* Dave Ramsey. 2017 https://www.daveramsey.com/baby-steps/6

Ramsey, Dave. *Baby Step 7.* Dave Ramsey. 2017
https://www.daveramsey.com/baby-steps/7

Rosenberg, Marshall. Nonviolent Communication.
PuddleDancer Press; Third Edition. 2015

Samuels J.F.; Bienvenu O.J.; Grados M.A.; Cullen
B.; Riddle M.A.; Liang K.; Eaton W.W.; Nestadt
G. *Prevalence and correlates of hoarding
behavior in a community-based sample.* Behaviour
Research and Therapy. 46: 836–844. 2008.

Scherhorn, G. The addictive trait in buying
behavior. Journal of Consumer Policy, 13(1), 33-
51. (1990).

Saxena, Sanjaya M.D. Brody Arthur L., M.D. et
al. Cerebral Glucose Metabolism in Obsessive-
Compulsive Hoarding. Psychiatry Online. 2004.

https://ajp.psychiatryonline.org/doi/pdf/10.1176/appi.ajp.161.6.1038

Singh, Satwant. *Helping Hoarders To Help Themselves.* Help For Hoarders. 2017. http://www.helpforhoarders.co.uk/self-help/

The Free Dictionary. Axis II. The Free Dictionary. 2018. https://medical-dictionary.thefreedictionary.com/Axis+II

The Mesquite Group. *Suggested or Ideal Spending Percentages.* The Mesquite Group. 2017. https://www.themesquitegroup.org/mg/mesquitegroup.nsf/a01caf1bfe0544248625729700305c6e/3ee6381e4606f8ff8525737a0063d03a/$FILE/Suggested+or+Ideal+Spending+Percentages.pdf

Tolin, David F., Randy O. Frost, and Gail Steketee. "An Open Trial of Cognitive-Behavioral Therapy for Compulsive Hoarding." Behaviour research and therapy 45.7 (2007): 1461–1470.

PMC. Web. 13 Sept. 2018. https://www.ncbi.nlm.nih.gov/pmc/articles/PMC1 950337/

Turner, M Cynthia, et al. The Clinician's Guide to Cognitive-Behavioral Therapy for Childhood Obsessive-compulsive Disorder. Science Direct. 2018. https://www.sciencedirect.com/book/9780128114 278

Tyler, Mara. *Shopping Addiction.* Health Line. 2016. https://www.healthline.com/health/addiction/shop ping

W. Black, D. Compulsive buying: A review. The Journal of clinical psychiatry. 57 Suppl 8. 50-4; discussion 55. 1996.

W. Black, Donald. A review of compulsive buying disorder. NCBI. 2007. https://www.ncbi.nlm.nih.gov/pmc/articles/PMC1805733/

Winestine MC. Compulsive shopping as a derivative of childhood seduction. Psychoanal Q. 1985;54:70–72.

Endnotes

[i] W. Black, Donald. A review of compulsive buying disorder. NCBI. 2007.
https://www.ncbi.nlm.nih.gov/pmc/articles/PMC1805733/
[ii] Black, Donald W., Martha Shaw, and Nancee Blum. "Pathological Gambling and Compulsive Buying: Do They Fall within an Obsessive-Compulsive Spectrum?" Dialogues in Clinical Neuroscience 12.2 175–185. Print. (2010)
[iii] W. Black, Donald. A review of compulsive buying disorder. NCBI. 2007.
https://www.ncbi.nlm.nih.gov/pmc/articles/PMC1805733/
[iv] W Black, D. Compulsive buying: A review. The Journal of clinical psychiatry. 57 Suppl 8. 50-4; discussion 55. 1996.
[v] Better Help. What Is Axis II Personality Disorder? Better Help. 2018.
https://www.betterhelp.com/advice/personality-disorders/what-is-axis-ii-personality-disorder/

[vi] The Free Dictionary. Axis II. The Free Dictionary. 2018. https://medical-dictionary.thefreedictionary.com/Axis+II

[vii] Tyler, Mara. *Shopping Addiction*. Health Line. 2016. https://www.healthline.com/health/addiction/shopping

[viii] Brewer, Judson A., and Marc N. Potenza. "The Neurobiology and Genetics of Impulse Control Disorders: Relationships to Drug Addictions." Biochemical pharmacology 75.1 (2008): 63–75. PMC. Web. 12 Sept. 2018.

[ix] Investopedia. *Compulsive Shopping*. Investopedia. 2017. https://www.investopedia.com/terms/c/compulsive-shopping.asp

[x] Addicion.com. Shopping Addiction. Addiction.com. 2018. https://www.addiction.com/addiction-a-to-z/shopping-addiction/

[xi] Scherhorn, G. The addictive trait in buying behavior. Journal of Consumer Policy, 13(1), 33-51. (1990).

[xii] Winestine MC. Compulsive shopping as a derivative of childhood seduction. Psychoanal Q. 1985;54:70–72.

[xiii] Holden C. Behavioral addictions; do they exist? Science. 2001;294:980–982.

[xiv] Schlosser S. Black D.W. Repertinger S, et al. Compulsive buying: demography, phenomenology, and comorbidity in 46 subjects. Gen Hosp Psychiatry. 1994;16:205–212.

[xv] Schlosser S. Black DW. Repertinger S, et al. Compulsive buying: demography, phenomenology, and comorbidity in 46 subjects. Gen Hosp Psychiatry. 1994;16:205–212.

[xvi] Miltenberger RG. Redlin J. Crosby R, et al. Direct and retrospective assessment of factors contributing to compulsive buying. J Behav Ther Exp Psychiatry. 2003;34:1–9.

[xvii] Christenson GA. Faber JR. de Zwann M. Compulsive buying: descriptive characteristics and psychiatric comorbidity. J Clin Psychiatry. 1994;55:5–11.

[xviii] Schlosser S. Black DW. Repertinger S, et al. Compulsive buying: demography, phenomenology, and comorbidity in 46 subjects. Gen Hosp Psychiatry. 1994;16:205–212.

[xix] Christenson GA. Faber JR. de Zwann M. Compulsive buying: descriptive characteristics and psychiatric comorbidity. J Clin Psychiatry. 1994;55:5–11.

[xx] Psychguides. Shopping Addiction Symptoms, Causes and Effects. Psychguides. 2018. https://www.psychguides.com/guides/shopping-addiction-symptoms-causes-and-effects/

[xxi] Illiades, Chris. Md. *How I stopped compulsive shopping.* Everyday Health. 2013. https://www.everydayhealth.com/depression/how-i-stopped-compulsive-shopping.aspx

[xxii] Rosenberg, Marshall. Nonviolent Communication. PuddleDancer Press; Third Edition. 2015.

[xxiii] International OCD Association. Diagnosing Hoarding Disorder. International OCD Association. 2013. https://hoarding.iocdf.org/professionals/diagnosing-hoarding-disorder/

[xxiv] Frank, Hannah & Stewart, Elyse & Walther, Michael & Benito, Kristen & Freeman, Jennifer & Conelea, Christine & Garcia, Abbe. (2013). Hoarding behavior among young children with obsessive–compulsive disorder. Journal of Obsessive-Compulsive and Related Disorders. 3. 10.1016/j.jocrd.2013.11.001.

[xxv] Turner, M Cynthia, et al. The Clinician's Guide to Cognitive-Behavioral Therapy for Childhood Obsessive-compulsive Disorder. Science Direct. 2018. https://www.sciencedirect.com/book/9780128114278

[xxvi] Turner, M Cynthia, et al. The Clinician's Guide to Cognitive-Behavioral Therapy for Childhood Obsessive-compulsive Disorder. Science Direct. 2018.

https://www.sciencedirect.com/book/978012811
4278

[xxvii] Pertusa A., Frost R.O., Fullana M. A., Samuels J., Steketee G., Tolin D., Saxena S., Leckman J.F., Mataix-Cols D. *Refining the boundaries of compulsive hoarding: A review.* Clinical Psychology Review. 30: 371–386. 2010.

[xxviii] American Psychiatric Association. *Hoarding Disorder*. American Psychiatric Association. 2013.

[xxix] Samuels J.F.; Bienvenu O.J.; Grados M.A.; Cullen B.; Riddle M.A.; Liang K.; Eaton W.W.; Nestadt G. *Prevalence and correlates of hoarding behavior in a community-based sample.* Behaviour Research and Therapy. 46: 836–844. 2008.

[xxx] Bratiotis, Christiana, PhD. Otte, Suzanne, MSW. Steketee, Gail, PhD. Muroff, Jordana, PhD. Frost, Randy O. PhD. *What is compulsive hoarding?* International OCD Foundation. 2009. https://iocdf.org/wp-content/uploads/2014/10/Hoarding-Fact-Sheet.pdf

[xxxi] Pertusa, Alberto M.D. Fullana Miguel A., Ph.D. Singh, Satwant M.Sc. Alonso, Pino M.D., Ph.D. Menchón, José M. M.D., Ph.D. Mataix-Cols David, Ph.D. Compulsive Hoarding: OCD Symptom, Distinct Clinical Syndrome, or Both? Psychiatry Online. 2008.

https://ajp.psychiatryonline.org/doi/pdfplus/10.1176/appi.ajp.2008.07111730

[xxxii] Pertusa, Alberto M.D. Fullana Miguel A., Ph.D. Singh, Satwant M.Sc. Alonso, Pino M.D., Ph.D. Menchón, José M. M.D., Ph.D. Mataix-Cols David, Ph.D Compulsive Hoarding: OCD Symptom, Distinct Clinical Syndrome, or Both? Psychiatry Online. 2008. https://ajp.psychiatryonline.org/doi/pdfplus/10.1176/appi.ajp.2008.07111730

[xxxiii] Howard Rosenthal, Human Services Dictionary p. 102. 2003.

[xxxiv] Saxena, Sanjaya M.D. Brody Arthur L., M.D. et al. Cerebral Glucose Metabolism in Obsessive-Compulsive Hoarding. Psychiatry Online. 2004. https://ajp.psychiatryonline.org/doi/pdf/10.1176/appi.ajp.161.6.1038

[xxxv] Jantz, Gregory L. Ph.D. *The Psychology Behind Hoarding*. Psychology Today. 2014. https://www.psychologytoday.com/blog/hope-relationships/201409/the-psychology-behind-hoarding

[xxxvi] Clinic, Mayo. Hoarding Disorder. Mayo Clinic. 2017. https://www.mayoclinic.org/diseases-conditions/hoarding-disorder/diagnosis-treatment/drc-20356062

[xxxvii] Tolin, David F., Randy O. Frost, and Gail Steketee. "An Open Trial of Cognitive-Behavioral Therapy for Compulsive Hoarding." Behaviour

research and therapy 45.7 (2007): 1461–1470. PMC. Web. 13 Sept. 2018. https://www.ncbi.nlm.nih.gov/pmc/articles/PMC 1950337/

[xxxviii] Singh, Satwant. *Helping Hoarders To Help Themselves.* Help For Hoarders. 2017. http://www.helpforhoarders.co.uk/self-help/

[xxxix] Berger, Vincent. Dr. *Spending and Shopping Addiction.* Psychologist Anywhere Anytime. 2005. http://www.psychologistanywhereanytime.com/ addiction_psychologist/psychologist_addiction_s pending.htm

[xl] Njeri Gitimu, Priscilla. Gitmu Waithaka, Abel. *Retail Therapy: Its relationship to Gender, Life Engagement, and Subjective Happiness (PDF).* Youngstown State University. 2017. http://www.documentshare.org/health-and-fitness/retail-therapy-its-relationship-to-gender-life-engagement-and-subjective-happiness/

[xli] Hartney, Elizabeth PhD. An Overview of Shopping Addiction. Verywell Mind. 2018. https://www.verywellmind.com/shopping-addiction-4157288

[xlii] Cruz, Veronica. *Impulse spending reduced if you get organized.* Market Business News. 2014. https://marketbusinessnews.com/impulse-spending-reduced-get-organized/12030

[xliii] American Psychological Association. American Psychological Association Survey Shows Money

Stress Weighing on Americans' Health Nationwide. American Psychological Association. 2015. http://www.apa.org/news/press/releases/2015/02/money-stress.aspx

[xliv] Klontz, Brad. Do You Have a Money Disorder? Psychology Today. 2010. https://www.psychologytoday.com/us/blog/mind-over-money/201001/do-you-have-money-disorder

[xlv] Klotz, Brad. Mind Over Money. Crown Business. 2009.

[xlvi] Mint. *The 50/20/30 Rule for Minimalist Budgeting*. Mint Life. 2016. https://blog.mint.com/saving/the-minimalist-guide-to-budgeting-in-your-20s-072016/

[xlvii] Mint. *The 50/20/30 Rule for Minimalist Budgeting*. Mint Life. 2016. https://blog.mint.com/saving/the-minimalist-guide-to-budgeting-in-your-20s-072016/

[xlviii] The Mesquite Group. *Suggested or Ideal Spending Percentages*. The Mesquite Group. 2017. https://www.themesquitegroup.org/mg/mesquitegroup.nsf/a01caf1bfe0544248625729700305c6e/3ee6381e4606f8ff8525737a0063d03a/$FILE/Suggested+or+Ideal+Spending+Percentages.pdf

[xlix] Dixon, Amanda. How Much Should I Spend on Rent? Smart Asset. 2018.

https://smartasset.com/mortgage/how-much-should-i-spend-on-rent

[l] Lendkey. *How Much of Your Income Should You Spend on Housing?* Lend Key. 2015. https://www.lendkey.com/blog/how-much-of-your-income-should-you-spend-on-housing/

[li] Comet. The Details of Debt. Comet. 2018. https://www.cometfi.com/details-of-debt

[lii] Ramsey, Dave. *Dave Ramsey's 7 Baby Steps*. Dave Ramsey. 2017. https://www.daveramsey.com/baby-steps

[liii] Ramsey, Dave. *Baby Step 1*. Dave Ramsey. 2017. https://www.daveramsey.com/baby-steps/1

[liv] Ramsey, Dave. *Baby Step 2*. Dave Ramsey. 2017. https://www.daveramsey.com/baby-steps/2

[lv] Ramsey, Dave. *Baby Step 3*. Dave Ramsey. 2017. https://www.daveramsey.com/baby-steps/3

[lvi] Ramsey, Dave. *Baby Step 4*. Dave Ramsey. 2017. https://www.daveramsey.com/baby-steps/4

[lvii] Ramsey, Dave. *Baby Step 5*. Dave Ramsey. 2017 https://www.daveramsey.com/baby-stcps/5

[lviii] Ramsey, Dave. *Baby Step 6*. Dave Ramsey. 2017 https://www.daveramsey.com/baby-steps/6

[lix] Ramsey, Dave. *Baby Step 7*. Dave Ramsey. 2017 https://www.daveramsey.com/baby-steps/7

[lx] Be More With Less. *Project 333*. Be More With Less. 2016. https://bemorewithless.com/project-333/

[lxi] Canning, Kristin. 6 Ways to Practice Hygge, the Danish Secret to Happiness. Health. 2017. https://www.health.com/mind-body/hygge

[lxii] Maines. Blueberry Muffins. Maines. 2018. https://www.maines.net/blueberry-muffins

[lxiii] Quinn, Erica. The True Cost of Eating Out Instead Of Cooking At Home. Investment Zen. 2017. http://www.investmentzen.com/news/the-true-cost-of-eating-out-instead-of-cooking-at-home/

[lxiv] USPS. Mailing and Shipping Prices. USPS. 2018. https://www.usps.com/business/prices.htm

50817401R00107

Made in the USA
Columbia, SC
11 February 2019